THE BLUE CLIFF RECORD

VOLUME TWO

The Blue Cliff Record

Translated from the Chinese *Pi Yen Lu* by
Thomas and J. C. Cleary

SHAMBHALA
Boulder & London
1977

SHAMBHALA PUBLICATIONS, INC.
1123 Spruce Street
Boulder, Colorado 80302

ISBN 0-87773-111-X
LCC 76-14202

Distributed in the United States by Random House
and in Canada by Random House of Canada Ltd.

Distributed in the Commonwealth by Routledge &
Kegan Paul Ltd., London and Henley-on-Thames

Printed in the United States of America

Contents

Biographical Supplement

Introduction

Zen stories and *koan* are not unique in form or content, nor in
their use as processes of concentration and transmission of
ways to enlightenment. The style and symbolism of *koan* do,
however, vary in different cultures where Chinese-derived Zen
existed, as well as from those of analogous Sufi, magical, and
mystical tales. The application of traditional lore in practice
seems to vary not only among 'religious traditions' but among
individual communities and students; this is only to be ex-
pected in light of the Zen emphasis on suiting the teachings to
the needs and capacities of those to be liberated.

In the introduction to volume one of *The Blue Cliff Record*,
a number of points in the history of Zen in China were touched
upon. There we emphasized the importance of the tenth and
eleventh century masters Yun Men Wen Yen and Fen Yang
Shan Chao in the development of the use of the *koan*, 'public
records' of sayings of ancient and contemporary teachers. It
should be pointed out that the quotation and elaboration of
Zen sayings is in evidence in the records of all the classical
masters who came to be regarded as the patriarchs of the five
schools and seven streams of Zen in China.

It was several centuries before Zen took root and grew in
Japan after its initial introduction; by the time of the numerous
Chinese emigrants and Japanese pilgrims who firmly established Zen in Japan in the second phase of its introduction in
the thirteenth and fourteenth centuries, the science of *koan*
use was well developed in China and was in fact an outstanding feature of Ch'an at that time. Emphasis on *koan* was new to
Japanese Buddhism but soon became a mainstay of Rinzai Zen
in particular. In sifting the vast repository of Zen literature for
hints on the nature and use of *koan*, therefore, it is reasonable
to turn to the medieval Japanese Zen masters who were experts
in this matter.

Daio Kokushi (Nanpo Jomyo 1235–1309), a famous Japanese
Zen master who traveled to China and was enlightened with
the guidance of Hsu T'ang Chih Yu (1185–1269), a master of

the lineage of Fen Yang and Yuan Wu, introduced the *koan* as he learned and experienced it in Sung China. He once said,

> *Although there are seventeen hundred* koan *in all, everything we see and hear—mountains, rivers, earth, plants, trees and forests—all are* koan, *the public matter.*
>
> *There are three levels of meaning in our school; merging with principle, working of activity, and transcendence.*[1] *The first, merging with principle, refers to the expressions of principle such as mind, nature, etc., spoken of by the Buddhas and ancestral teachers of Zen. Next, the workings of action refers to the Buddhas and ancestors really expressing compassion, 'twisting their noses' and 'blinking their eyes,' as it were, saying things like 'a clay ox flies through the sky, a stone horse plunges into the river.'*
>
> *After that, transcendence refers to the direct speech of the Buddhas and ancestors, the real character of all things, etc., where nothing is different; 'sky is sky, earth is earth, mountains are mountains, rivers are rivers'; 'the eyes are horizontal, the nose is vertical'—such sayings refer to this.*
>
> *However, to pass through these three phrases is hard. Some may stop in principle and produce interpretation and understanding, knowledge and opinion, to understand the principle elucidated in the written and spoken teachings.*
>
> *Some may go along with workings of action in a flurry and not completely cut off doubt. They stay one-sidedly in the exercise of possibilities. Some abide in transcendence, maintain the view that everything is actually so; they thus fall into the realm of unconcern.*[2]

The ancient model of this 'classification' of *koan* and stages of practice could be said to be Pai Chang's 'three phases' (or 'phrases'), summarized in the biographical extract on Pai Chang in volume one of *The Blue Cliff Record*, these three phases, or phrases—referring to phases of expression as a method of teaching—are stages of practice and realization; detachment, calm, and personal liberation in the first phase, not abiding in detachment in the second phase, and having no understanding of nonabiding in the third phase. Pai Chang said that all the teachings of Buddhism have these three stages, and they represent a historical scheme, not only of the personal experience of people working on Zen, but of communities and constellations of communities, including their verbal and written expressions. Moreover, Pai Chang says that Buddhahood is beyond these stages and even refers to a saying in a scripture likening this to a deer leaping thrice getting out of the net.

Later Lin Chi spoke of three essentials and three mysteries; what exactly this meant in terms of Lin Chi's dealings with his disciples is one of those issues which remains obscure in spite of a number of verses by later teachers alluding to meditative states, but it should be clear that each of Pai Chang's three phases apply to each of the other phases; none of the succeeding ones can be reached without realizing the preceding one, but in each stage there are one-sided and integrated realization both. That is, for example, at the first level of detachment, a tacit negation of everything by cultivation of indifference and equanimity, utter dispassion. Detachment from detachment does not see the world as hateful or personal extinction as desirable; not dwelling on anything, even detachment, therefore, is real detachment; but unless one has actually realized detachment in (what is now seen as) the one-sided way, in the 'relative within the absolute,' or relative absolute way, so-called detachment from detachment is a feeble excuse at best. Without belaboring this point further, it can be seen that each phase must ultimately integrate with the others in the development of Zen practice.[3]

Centuries later Hakuin (1686–1769) and his disciples and heirs further developed systematic *koan* form and use. The principal type *koan* were referred to as Dharmakaya, or body of reality *koan*; they concentrated on the formless aspect first, to rid the mind of all preconceptions based on long accumulation of habit. The next stage was called workings of activity, referring to re-emergence into life after the great death, with the mind clean and mirrorlike. Ultimately the 'mirror' can function in a multifaceted way, each facet reflecting the other facets of the essential unity of the jewel-mirror, but originally it does not discriminate and define anything in a fixed way, coming into the realm of 'one state, one object,' seeming both unique and differentiated, constantly changing, one object now encompassing the universe, the universe now appearing as one object.

It would seem that the earlier 'workings of action' stage was refined by Hakuin into the 'workings of action,' 'verbal expression,' and 'difficult to pass through.' Just as the study of verbal expression is the third phase of study in the Hakuin school, the ancient Ts'ao Shan said of the third of the five ranks of Tung Shan, "coming from within the absolute is words within the wordless." Ts'ao Shan also said, however, "in each phrase there are no words; they do not set up what is precious, and do not fall into either side—that is why it is called coming from the absolute." This is coming from the absolute state to express it in relative terms which do not violate the absolute, thus allowing one to discern the unspoken message without clinging to partial views about the overt meanings of the words, but rather using those meanings only as a channel of attention.

Hakuin's fourth stage, 'difficult to pass through,' corresponds to Tung Shan's 'attainment within the relative,' the stage of the 'lotus blooming in the fire,' one adept in darkness and adept in light, the tantric master who balances wisdom and compassion.

The fifth stage of Hakuin's system, working with Tung Shan's five ranks of relative and absolute interrelating, corresponds to Daio's 'transcendence,' and Tung Shan's simultaneous arrival within both (relative and absolute), what Ts'ao Shan called mutual integration. In the modern system, the five ranks include certain specific koan, especially Tung Shan's verses, but are also a mirror in which all the experiences one has realized can be seen. It is that, as Hakuin said, which smashes the twin void (of the 'lotus' and the 'fire'); that is why it is called transcendence.

But then, as it is said, there is an impassable gate at the final barrier; it is also said there is a road going beyond of which none of the sages have told. Therefore a discussion of the mortal life, of living a life of cause in spite of the fact that one has seen everything, of discipline that is efficiency in action and strength of body and intent in the struggle for enlightenment of all beings, is given after the student's eyes have been opened, as it had been given in the beginning to instill the mind with the spirit of enlightenment.

Regarding the matter of self-help and helping others as it relates to *koan* study, in Zen it is sometimes said that one who has not yet penetrated should seek the meaning, while one who has penetrated should seek the phrase, or expression. Someone asked Zen master Muso (1275–1352), who was also a kokushi, or Teacher of the Nation, about the difference between investigating the meaning, or intent, and investigating the expression, or phrase. Muso said,

> *Meaning and phrase are terms which come from poetry. When discussing Japanese poems, for example, it is like saying that a verse has nice phraseology but the sentiment it conveys is crude. In Zen we have gates of teaching called meaning and phrase, borrowing those terms; though the words are the same, the meaning is different.*
>
> *In Zen, there are various teachings such as transcendence and return, That Side (the 'other side') and This Side, holding still and letting go, capturing and releasing, killing and reviving, three mysteries, three essentials, five positions of lord and minister; these are phrases. Among students of trivia, there are those who think that to clearly know the distinctions among these teachings is called attainment of meaning and to be able to explain and discuss them with others freely is what is called attainment of expression. What these people think is meaning is still in the sphere of the phrase.*
>
> *Discussing principles of holding still and letting go, assessing the transcendent or the imminent within the spoken phrase, is called investigating the phrase; even when sitting silently facing a wall, if you harbor various mixtures of knowledge and understanding in your heart, figuring and calculating, this is still investigating the phrase.*

*Therefore, the method of having people investigate
the meaning is to have them cast off all understanding and emotional assessments and look at
a* koan *directly. Even while reading the records of
words of the ancients or hearing the teachings of
a guide, if you directly forget what is on your
mind and do not create an intellectual understanding about sense or principle, this is investigating the meaning.*

Once *a student has clearly awakened to the meaning of the ancestors, then a teacher may discuss
with him the differences in style of the five
schools of Zen, and deal with the methods and
modes of holding still, letting go, capturing, releasing, killing, giving life, praising and censuring, etc.—if one does not successfully investigate
these expressions, he cannot teach people; that is
why an ancient who had realized the truth was
told that not to doubt verbal expressions is a
great illness.*

The practice of intense concentration on a koan, complete ab-
sorption in the so-called 'mass of doubt' generated while gazing
at the saying, seems to have become widely used in Rinzai Zen.
Muso said, "If a student has any seeking for enlightenment in
his mind, he is not really keeping a koan before him." Another
great Rinzai master, Shoitsu Kokushi (1202–1280) said,

*In the direct teaching of the ancestral teachers there
are no special methods; cast off all entangle-
ments, lay to rest all affairs, and for three hours
in the morning and three hours at night keep
watch over the tip of your nose. When you drift
into distinctions among things, just call a saying
to mind—do not think in terms of Buddhism, or
of getting rid of anything; don't consciously
await understanding, don't let feelings or intellect create doubtful unrest. With no road of reason, no taste, like an iron bun, cut directly in
with a single stroke without getting involved in
various ideas. After a long time like this you will*

*naturally be like awakening from a dream, like a
lotus flower blooming. At this moment the saying you have been concentrating on is like a piece
of tile used to knock on a door; throw it away on
the 'other side,' and then look at the words of the
Buddhas and ancestors illustrating the workings
of active capacity. These are all only to stop a
child's crying. The one road of transcendence
going beyond does not let anything more
through, but cuts off the essential pass of ordinary and holy.*

Simply sitting, with ultimate if tacit faith in the inherent enlightenment of the original mind, transcending the forces of
habitual illusion by attrition, is usually associated with Soto
Zen, especially as taught by the famous Dogen, but the same
'art' was also taught by Rinzai masters like Shoitsu. The use
of *koan* concentration as a 'secondary' measure, to focus the
wandering mind as described by Shoitsu here, was also taught
by such leading Zen masters as Keizan and Meiho, who greatly
influenced the development of Soto Zen in the fourteenth century. However, intense concentration in this way evidently can
have negative results if improperly tuned, according to the Soto
Zen master Gesshu, who like Hakuin was a powerful force in
the premodern revival of Zen in Japan:

*When I was staying in Choenji in Mikawa a long
time ago, I gave various koan to the students and
made them work on them, but very few people
got koan totally solidly in their grasp to reach the
realm of great awakening and great penetration.
Most people just carried the koan around—for
some this brought about pain in the chest, some
became depressed and consumptive; or else they
produced all sorts of conceptualizations to make
rational understanding, just going further and
further from the fundamental meaning of the
koan, and got bored besides.*
*When the real true overwhelming doubt arises,
keeping one koan constantly whether awake or
sleeping for even seven days, not affected by any-*

*thing, it just becomes one solid state—then joy
rises ceaselessly in your mind. As soon as this
state of mind arises, it already becomes a seed of
wisdom, and you will not regress in your deter-
mination for enlightenment.*

From the sayings of these Zen masters we can see that 'this
side' and 'that side,' rational understanding and the ordinary
world, reflections of reflections, and, engulfing all that, the
mirror itself, inconceivable in light as well as darkness, all
have a place in Zen expression and experience. The observation
of some *koan* involves 'looking back' into the source of consciousness and thought, until all impulses are ended or over-
come; this is supposed to lead to *nirvana*, the 'great death,'
leaving one equanimous by experiencing relative equanimity,
indifference, as nothingness itself, the opposite of existence in
thought and deed.

Forms of asceticism, standards of conduct, ritual remember-
ance, various auxiliary practices, as well as *zazen*, sitting meditation, the main practice of Zen monasteries, are not only intentional approaches to this extinction of personal egoism and
the concomitant experience of pure clarity, wishlessness,
openness, without any design. These are also, after all, expressions of solidarity with the human world, even as a bequest for
some unforseen future; hence they are not necessarily con-
nected or disconnected from knowledge and vision of reality
only by tradition in the purely social or conventional institu-
tional sense.

The unity of body and mind is often emphasized by Bud-
dhists, but the famous 'body-mind duality' of Western
philosophy is indeed sadly borne out by many of the social,
intellectual, economic, and animal habits of human beings,
especially among certain socio-strategic groups in times of
plenty and little. So on a personal level the search of the renun-
ciant for peace in having few desires and being content is a
prelude to experiences truly beyond mundane knowledge or
cares, but as an outward feature it stands for civilization in the
human community, even if it be embryonic compared to the
worlds of Mahayana, the great vehicle, or of the scenes of the
tantric *mandalas* or Zen *koan*. These pure lands are already

there, here within us, awaiting discovery; to pull out the weeds and cut through the brambles, *koan* like the word 'No' or 'Who' or 'What' are often repeated.

Once the person seeking reality has experienced the overwhelming death and complete stillness and calm, it is necessary 'to know not only that the needle is sharp, but also that the chisel is square,' to have both wisdom and knowledge, so that 'each branch of coral holds the moon.' This is a way of translating what one has realized into active expression to help others become enlightened with what means are available while deepening one's knowledge in and for that very task. The 'one road going beyond, which the sages didn't transmit' mentioned so many times in *The Blue Cliff Record* is a classic 'turning word' illustrating the 'multiplicity within one' and 'nonduality in two' of Zen; it does not refer only to the inexpressible absolute, host within host, the experience of the absolute state as the extinction of the sense of self, life, and so forth, resulting in the end of self-conscious suffering. The word for transcendence also means, in vernacular, progress; here it is in the sense of the need for the successor to go beyond the teacher for the teaching to really be handed on, to provide 'a beacon for future generations.' Here they say that there is nothing to be transmitted, but to approach that nothing is difficult and deadly, virtually impossible to survive without what we might call the compassion of the Buddhas, enlightened ancestors.

Sadaparibhuta, an ancient bodhisattva whose story is told in the *Saddharmapundarika*, or Lotus of the Truth scripture, used to say to people that he did not dislike them or hold anything against them, because they would all eventually become Buddhas. After a while people began to dislike him for saying this, so he had to learn more. An ancient Zen master in China used to say 'this mind is Buddha,' until people stopped awakening and began to think they 'had' Buddha; then the master said, 'not mind, not Buddha.' These Ch'an sayings compiled in *The Blue Cliff Record* are means which the ancients devised to offset this bewildering bluntness, to help us find the inconceivable infinite right before us without being bogged down in customary doubts and considerations on one hand or being burnt to a cinder in the fire of trascendent wisdom without properly preparing the vessel.

NOTES

1. In the book *The Zen Koan* (or *Zen Dust*) by Isshu Miura and Ruth F. Sasaki can be found different translations of the terms used here and a discussion of *koan* practice in the Hakuin school of Rinzai Zen. (see *The Blue Cliff Record* vol. I)

2. This and other quotes in the introduction are translated from sermons of famous Japanese Zen masters compiled by Kuruma Takudo in his *Zenshu Seiten*, or Zen Bible (Kyoto, Heiryakuji Shoten, 1961).

3. Pai Chang's three phases could be understood as being applied to themselves, as three phases of each of the same three phases; Lin Chi's three mysteries and three essentials seem to be developments of this; detachment, nonabiding, and nonintellectualization are each an aspect of detachment, nonabiding, and nonintellectualization. The later definition of three stages of realization of principles, active application, and transcendence, also comes from this.

Ch'ang Sha Wandering in the Mountains

CASE

One day Ch'ang Sha went wandering in the mountains. Upon returning, when he got to the gate,[1] the head monk asked, "Where are you coming from, Master?"[2]

Sha said, "From wandering in the mountains."[3]

The head monk asked, "Where did you go?"[4]

Sha said, "First I went pursuing the fragrant grasses; then I returned following the falling flowers."[5]

The head monk said, "How very much like the sense of springtime."[6]

Sha said, "It even surpasses the autumn dew[a] dripping on the lotuses."[7] Hsueh Tou added the remark, "Thanks for your reply."[8]

NOTES

1. Today, one day. He has only fallen into the weeds; at first he was falling into the weeds; later he was still falling in the weeds.
2. He still wants to try this old fellow. The arrow has flown past Korea.
3. Don't fall in the weeds. He's suffered quite a loss. A man in the weeds.
4. A thrust. If he had gone anywhere, he couldn't avoid falling into the weeds. They drag each other into a pit of fire.
5. He's let slip quite a bit. From the beginning he's just been sitting in a forest of thorns.
6. He comes following along, adding error to error; one hand uplifts, one hand presses down.
7. He adds mud to dirt. The first arrow was light; the second arrow was deep. What end will there ever be?
8. A group of fellows playing with a mud ball. The three have their crimes listed on the same indictment.

COMMENTARY

Great Master Chao Hsien of the Deer Park at Ch'ang Sha succeeded to the Dharma of Nan Ch'uan; he was a contemporary
of Chao Chou and Tzu Hu. The point of his wit was sharp and
swift. If anyone asked about the Teachings, he would then give
him an explanation of the Teachings; if someone wanted a
verse, he would then give a verse. If you wanted to have a
meeting of adepts, then he would have a meeting of adepts
with you.

Yang Shan was usually considered foremost in having a
sharp intellect. Once as he was enjoying the moon along with
Ch'ang Sha, Yang Shan pointed at the moon and said,
"Everyone has this; it's just that they can't use it." Sha said,
"Quite true. So, shall I have you use it?" Yang Shan said, "Try
to use it yourself." Sha kicked him over with one blow. Yang
Shan got up and said, "Respected Uncle, you are just like a
tiger." Hence, people later called Ch'ang Sha "Ts'en the Tiger."

One day as Sha returned from a stroll in the mountains, the
head monk, who was also a man of Sha's congregation, asked
him, "Where are you coming from, Master?" Sha said, "I come
from a stroll in the mountains." The head monk asked, "Where
did you go?" Sha said, "First I went following the fragrant
grasses; then I returned pursuing the falling flowers." Only a
man who had cut off the ten directions could be like this. The
Ancients, in leaving and entering, never ever failed to be mindful of this Matter. See how the host and guest shift positions
together; confronting the situation directly, neither overlaps
the other. Since he was wandering in the mountains, why did
the monk ask, "Where did you go?" If he had been one of
today's followers of Ch'an, he would have said, "I came to the
inn on Mount Chia." See how that man of old did not have
even the slightest hair of reason or judgement, and that he had
no place to abide: that is why he said, "First I went following
the fragrant grasses; then I returned pursuing the falling flowers." The head monk then followed his idea and said to him
"How very much like the sense of springtime!" Sha said, "It
even surpasses the autumn dew dripping on the lotuses."
Hsueh Tou says on behalf (of the monk), "Thanks for your
reply," as the final word. This too falls on both sides but ultimately does not remain on either side.

In the past there was a scholar, Chang Ch'o, who upon reading the *Sutra of the Thousand Names of Buddha*, asked, "Of the hundreds and thousands of Buddhas, I have only heard their names; what lands do they dwell in, and do they convert beings or not?" Ch'ang Sha said, "Since Ts'ui Hao[b] wrote his poems in the Golden Crane Pavillion, have you ever written or not?" Ch'o said, "No." Sha said, "When you have some free time, you should write one."

Ts'en the Tiger's usual way of helping people was like jewels turning, gems revolving; he wanted people to understand immediately on the face of it. The verse says,

VERSE

The earth is clear of any dust—
> Open wide the doors and windows—who is under the eaves? None can miss this. The world is at peace.

Whose eyes do not open?
> One must emit a great radiant light from his forehead before this is possible. Why scatter dirt and sand?

First he went following the fragrant grasses,
> He's slipped quite a bit. It's not just one instance of falling into the weeds. Fortunately it happens that he already said this before.

Then he returned pursuing the falling flowers.
> Everywhere is completely real. Luckily he came back. Under his feet the mud is three feet deep.

A weary crane[c] alights on a withered tree,
> Accompanying him left and right, he adds a phrase. Still there are so many idle concerns?

A mad monkey cries on the ancient terrace.
> After all it depends on personal application of effort. It is impossible either to add a phrase or to take a phrase away.

Ch'ang Sha's boundless meaning—
> I strike. What does the final phrase say? Bury them all in one pit. He's fallen into the ghost cave.

Bah!

A man in the weeds; this is drawing the bow after the thief has gone. Still, he can't be let go.

COMMENTARY

Take this public case along with Yang Shan's asking a monk, "Where have you just come from?" The monk said, "Mount Lu." Yang Shan said, "Did you visit the Five Elders Peak?" The monk said, "I didn't get there." Yang Shan said, "You never visited the mountain at all." Distinguish the black and white, and see if they are the same or if they are different. At this point, mental machinations must come to an end, and conscious knowledge be forgotten, so that over mountains, rivers, and earth, plants, people, and animals you have no leaking at all. If you are not like this, the Ancients called that "still remaining in the realm of surpassing wonder."

Haven't you seen how Yun Men said, "Even if you realize that there is no trouble at all in the mountains, rivers, and earth, still this is a turning phrase: when you do not see any forms, this is only half the issue. You must further realize that there is a time when the whole thing is brought up, the single opening upward; only then can you sit in peace?" If you can pass through, then as before mountains are mountains, rivers are rivers; each abides in its own state, each occupies its own body. You will be like a completely blind man. Chao Chou said,

> The cock crows in the early morning;
> Sadly I see as I rise how worn out I am;
> I haven't a kilt or a shirt,
> Just the semblance of a robe.
> My loincloth has no seat, my pants no opening—
> On my head are three or five pecks of grey ashes.
> Originally I intended to practice to help save others;
> Who would have suspected that instead I would
>   become an idiot?

If one can truly reach this realm, whose eyes would not open? Though you go through upsets and spills, all places are this realm, all places are this time and season. "The ten directions

are without walls, and the four quarters are without gates."
That is why he said, "First I went following the fragrant grasses; then I returned pursuing the falling flowers." Skillful indeed, Hsueh Tou just goes and adds a phrase to his left and a
phrase to his right, just like a poem. "The weary crane alights
on a withered tree. The mad monkey cries on an ancient terrace." When Hsueh Tou has drawn it out this far, he realizes
how he has indulged himself: suddenly he says, "Ch'ang Sha's
boundless meaning—Bah!" This was like having a dream but
suddenly awakening. Though Hsueh Tou gave a shout, he still
didn't completely finish the matter. If it were up to me, I would
do otherwise: Ch'ang Sha's boundless meaning—dig out the
ground and bury it deeper.

TRANSLATORS' NOTES

a. According to Tenkei Denson, the head monk thought there was
    still some warmth, but Ch'ang Sha is saying No, it's clear and
    cool, colder than the autumn dew.
b. Ts'ui Hao was a statesman of the Northern Wei dynasty, noted for
    his sagacity, who also composed literary works. Golden Crane
    Pavillion was in Hupeh west of Wu Ch'ang, so situated as to look
    out over a vast vista.
c. The crane is associated with longevity.

P'an Shan's There Is Nothing in the World

POINTER

It is futile effort to linger in thought over the action of a lightning bolt: when the sound of thunder fills the sky, you will hardly have time to cover your ears. To unfurl the red flag of victory over your head, whirl the twin swords behind your ears—if not for a discriminating eye and a familiar hand, how could anyone be able to succeed?

Some people lower their heads and linger in thought, trying to figure it out with their intellect. They hardly realize that they are seeing ghosts without number in front of their skulls.

Now tell me, without falling into intellect, without being caught up in gain or loss, when suddenly there is such a demonstration to awaken you, how will you reply? To test, I cite this to see.

CASE

P'an Shan imparted the words which said, "There is nothing in the triple world;[1] where can mind be found?"[2]

NOTES

1. Once the arrow has left the bowstring, it has no power to come back. The moon's brightness shines, revealing the night traveller. He has hit the mark. One who knows the law fears it. He ought to have been hit before he finished talking.
2. Best not fool people! It's not worth bringing up again. Examine for yourself. Immediately striking, I would say, "What is this?"

COMMENTARY

Master Pao Chi of Mount P'an in Yu Chou in the far north was
a venerable adept succeeding to Ancestor Ma. Later he produced one man, P'u Hua. When the Master was about to pass
on, he said to the community, "Is there really anyone who can
depict my true likeness?" The people all drew likenesses and
presented them to the Master. The Master scolded every one of
them. P'u Hua came forth and said, "I can depict it." The
Master said, "Why do you not show it to me?" P'u Hua immediately turned a somersault and left. The Master said, "Later on, this guy will appear crazy to teach others."

One day, he said to the community, "There is nothing in the
triple world; where can mind be found? The elements are basically empty; how can a Buddha abide? The polar star does not
move; quiet and still, without traces, once presented face to
face, there is no longer anything else."

Hsueh Tou takes up two phrases and eulogizes them; this
here is raw gold, a rough jewel. Have you not heard it said,
"Curing illness does not depend on a donkey-load of
medicine." Why do I say I would have hit him before he finished speaking? Just because he was wearing stocks, giving
evidence of his crimes.

An Ancient said, "When you hear mention of the phrase
beyond sound, do not go seeking it in your mind." But tell me,
what was his meaning? Just like a rushing stream crossing a
sword; thunder rolls, a comet flies. If you hesitate and seek it in
thought, even though a thousand Buddhas appeared in the
world, you would grope around without finding them. But if
you are one who has deeply entered the inner sanctum, pierced
the bone and pierced the marrow, seen all the way through,
then P'an Shan will have suffered a loss. If you are smeared
with mud and dripping with water, turning about on the pile of
sound and form, you have still never seen P'an Shan even in a
dream. My late master Wu Tsu said, "Pass beyond the Other
Side, and only then will you have any freedom."

Have you not seen how the Third Patriarch said, "Grasp it,
and you lose balance and surely enter a false path. Let go naturally; there is neither going nor abiding in essence." If here you
say that there is neither Buddha nor Dharma, still you have

gone into a ghost cave. The Ancients called this the Deep Pit of Liberation. Originally it was a good causal basis, but it brings on a bad result. That is why it is said that a non-doing, unconcerned man is still oppressed by golden chains. Still, you must have penetrated all the way to the bottom before you will realize it. If you can say what cannot be said, can do what cannot be done, this is called the place of turning the body. There is nothing in the triple world; where can mind be found? If you make an intellectual interpretation, you will just die at his words; Hsueh Tou's view is piercing and penetrating. Thus he versifies:

VERSE

There is nothing in the triple world;
   The words are still in our ears.

Where can mind be found?
   It is not worth the trouble to mention again. See for yourself. I strike and say, "What is this?"

The white clouds form a canopy;
   Adding a head to a head. A thousand layers, ten thousand layers.

The flowing spring makes a lute—
   Do you hear it? They come along with each other. Each hearing is enough to lament.

One tune, two tunes; no one understands.
   It does not fall into A or B; it has nothing to do with D or E. He is going by a side road. The five sounds and six notes are all distinctly clear. Take what's yours and get out. When you hear it, you go deaf.

When the rain has passed, the autumn water is deep in the evening pond.
   The thunder is so swift, there's no time to cover the ears. After all he's dragging in mud and dripping with water. Where is he? Immediately I strike.

COMMENTARY

"There is nothing in the triple world; where can mind be found?" Hsueh Tou makes a verse which resembles the Flower Garland Cosmos.[a] Some people say he sings it out from the midst of nothingness, but anyone with his eyes open would never understand in this way. Hsueh Tou goes to (P'an Shan's) side and drapes two phrases on him, saying, "The white clouds form a canopy; the flowing spring makes a lute."

When Su Tung P'o, scholar of the Imperial Han Lin Academy, saw Chao Chueh, he made a verse which said,

> *The sound of the valley stream is itself the Vast*
> *Eternal Tongue;*
> *Are not the colors of the mountains the Pure Body?*
> *Since evening, eighty-four thousand verses;*
> *Another day, how could I quote them to others?*

Hsueh Tou borrows the flowing spring to make a long tongue; that is why he says, "No one understands." The harmony of this tune requires you to be a connoisseur before you can appreciate it. If you are not such a person, it is useless to take the trouble to incline an ear to it. An Ancient said, "Even a deaf man can sing a foreign song; good or bad, high or low, he doesn't hear at all." Yun Men said, "When it is raised, if you do not pay attention, you will miss it; if you want to think about it, in what aeon will you ever awaken?" Raising is the essence, paying attention is the function; if you can see before it is brought up, before any indications are distinguishable, then you will occupy the essential bridge; if you can see at the moment when the indications are distinguishable, then you will have shining and function. If you see after the indications are distinct, you will fall into intellection.

Hsueh Tou is exceedingly compassionate, and goes on to say to you, "When the rain has passed, the autumn water is deep in the evening pond." This verse has been discussed and judged by someone who praised Hsueh Tou for having the talent of a Han Lin scholar.[b] "The rain passed, the autumn water is deep in the evening pond." Still you must set eyes on it quickly; if you tarry in doubt, then you will look without seeing.

TRANSLATORS' NOTES

a. The Flower Garland Cosmos, where all are in each and each is in all, as set out in the *Hua Yen Sutra.*

b. During T'ang times the dynasty established the Han Lin "Academy" to draw on the services of talented literary men. To have the ability of a Han Lin scholar means to have superlative talent.

Feng Hsueh's Workings of the Iron Ox[a]

POINTER

If we discuss the gradual, it is going against the ordinary to merge with the Way: in the midst of a bustling market place, seven ways up and down and eight ways across.

If we discuss the sudden, it doesn't leave a hint of a trace; a thousand sages cannot find it.

If, on the other hand, we do not set up sudden or gradual, then what? To a quick person, one word; to a quick horse, one blow of the whip. At such a time, who is the master? As a test, I cite this to see.

CASE

At the government headquarters in Ying Chou, Feng Hsueh entered the hall and said,[1] "The Patriarchal Masters' Mind Seal is formed like the workings of the Iron Ox:[2a] when taken away, the impression remains;[3] when left there, then the impression is ruined.[4] But if neither removed nor left there,[5] is sealing right or is not sealing right?"[6]

At that time there was a certain Elder Lu P'i who came forth and said, "I have the workings of the Iron Ox:[7] please, Teacher, do not impress the seal."[8]

Hsueh said, "Accustomed to scouring the oceans fishing for whales, I regret to find instead a frog crawling in the muddy sand."[9]

P'i stood there thinking.[10] Hsueh shouted and said, "Elder, why do you not speak further?"[11] P'i hesitated;[12] Hsueh hit him with his whisk.[13] Hsueh said, "Do you still remember the words? Try to quote them."[14] As P'i was about to open his mouth,[15] Hsueh hit him again with his whisk.

The Governor said, "The Buddhist Law and the Law of Kings are the same."[16]

Hsueh said, "What principle have you seen?"[17]

The Governor said, "When you do not settle what is to be settled, instead you bring about disorder."[18]

Hseuh thereupon descended from his seat.[19]

NOTES

1. He explains Ch'an in public; what is he saying?
2. Thousands of people, ten thousands of people cannot budge it. Where is the impenetrable difficulty? The seal of the three essentials opens, without running afoul of the point.
3. The true imperative must be carried out. Wrong!
4. A second offense is not permitted. Observe the time when the imperative is being carried out. A thrust! Immediately I strike.
5. See how there is no place to put it. How difficult to understand!
6. The heads of everyone in the world appear and disappear. The design is already showing. But I only ask that you turn over the meditation seat and disperse the great assembly with shouts.
7. He's fished out one who's "awakened in the dark." Nevertheless, he's unusual.
8. Good words; nevertheless, he's wrong.
9. Like a falcon catching a pigeon. His jewel net extends throughout space. The wonder horse runs a thousand miles.
10. What a pity! Still, there's a place for him to show himself; what a pity to let it go.
11. He captures the flag and steals the drum. The boiling turmoil has come.
12. Three times he has died. A double case.
13. Well struck! This order requires such a man to carry it out.
14. What is the need? He adds frost upon snow.
15. Once having died, he won't come to life again. This fellow makes others out to be fools. He has run into (Feng Hsueh's) poison hand.
16. Clearly. After all, they've been seen through by a bystander.
17. He too gives a good thrust; he has turned the spearpoint around and come back with it.
18. He seems to be right, but he's not really right. (Still,) you must realize that the bystander has eyes. When someone of the eastern house dies, someone of the western house helps in the mourning.
19. He adds error to error. Seeing the situation, he adjusts. Now the task of study is completed.

COMMENTARY

Feng Hsueh was a venerable adept in the lineage of Lin Chi.

First Lin Chi was in Huang Po's community. As he was planting pine trees, Huang Po said to him, "Deep in the mountains here, why plant so many pine trees?" Chi said, "For one thing, to provide scenery for the monastery; second, to make a signpost for people of later generations." Having spoken, he hoed the ground once. Po said, "Although you are right, you have already suffered twenty blows of my staff." Chi struck the ground one more time and whistled under his breath. Po said, "With you, my school will greatly flourish in the world."

Che of Ta Kuei said, "Lin Chi in his way seemed to invite trouble in a peaceful area; nevertheless, only when immutable in the face of danger can one be called a real man."

Huang Po said, "My school, coming to you, will greatly flourish in the world." He seems to be fond of his child, unaware of being unseemly.

Later, Kuei Shan asked Yang Shan, "Did Huang Po at that time only entrust his bequest to Lin Chi alone, or is there yet anyone else?" Yang Shan said, "There is, but the age is so remote that I do not want to mention it to you, Master." Kuei Shan said, "Although you are right, I still want to know; just mention it and let's see." Yang Shan said, "One man will point south; in Wu-yueh the order will be carried out, and coming to a great wind, then it will stop." This foretold of Feng Hsueh ("Wind Cave").

Feng Hsueh first studied with Hsueh Feng for five years. As it happened, he asked for help with this story: "As Lin Chi entered the hall, the head monks of both halls simultaneously shouted. A monk asked Lin Chi, 'Are there guest and host, or not?' Chi said, 'Guest and host are evident.'" Feng Hsueh asked, "What is the inner meaning of this?" Hsueh Feng said, "In the past I went along with Yen T'ou or Ch'in Shan to see Lin Chi; on the way, we heard he had already passed on. If you want to understand his talk about guest and host, you should call upon venerable adepts in the stream of his school."

One day he finally saw Nan Yuan. He recited the preceding story and said, "I have come especially to see you personally." Nan Yuan said, "Hsueh Feng is an Ancient Buddha."

One time he saw Ching Ch'ing. Ch'ing asked him, "Where have you just come from?" Hsueh said, "I come from the East." Ch'ing said, "And did you cross the little (Ts'ao) river?" Hsueh said, "The great ship sails alone through the sky; there are no little rivers to cross." Ch'ing said, "Birds cannot fly across mirror lake and picture mountain; have you not merely overheard another's remark?" Hsueh said, "Even the sea fears the power of a warship; sails flying through the sky, it crosses the five lakes." Ch'ing raised his whisk and said, "What about this?" Hsueh said, "What is this?" Ch'ing said, "After all, you don't know." Hsueh said, "Appearing, disappearing, rolling up and rolling out, I act the same as you, Teacher." Ch'ing said, "Casting auguring sticks, you listen to the empty sound; fast asleep, you are full of gibberish." Hsueh said, "When a marsh is wide, it can contain a mountain; a cat can subdue a leopard." Ch'ing said, "I forgive your crime and pardon your error; you better leave quickly." Hsueh said, "If I leave, I lose." Then he went out; when he got to the Dharma Hall, he said to himself, "Big man, the case is not yet finished; how then can you quit?" Then he turned around and went into the abbot's room. As Ching Ch'ing sat there, Hsueh asked, "I have just now offered my ignorant view and insulted your venerable countenance; humbly favored by the Teacher's compassion, I have not yet been given punishment for my crime." Ching Ch'ing said, "Just awhile ago you said you came from the East: did you not come from Ts'ui Yen?" Hsueh said, "Hsueh Tou actually lies east of Pao Kai." Ching Ch'ing said, "If you don't chase the lost sheep, crazy interpretations cease. Instead you come here and recite poems." Hsueh said, "When you meet a swordsman on the road, you should show your sword; do not offer poetry to one who is not a poet." Ch'ing said, "Put the poetry away right now and try to use your sword a little." Hsueh said, "A decapitated man carried the sword away." Ch'ing said, "You not only violate the method of the teaching; you also show your own fat-headedness." Hsueh said, "Unless I violate the method of the teaching, how could I awaken to the mind of an Ancient Buddha?" Ch'ing said, "What do you call the mind of an Ancient Buddha?" Hsueh said, "Again you grant your allowance; now what do you have, Teacher?" Ch'ing said, "This patch-robed one from the East cannot distinguish beans from wheat. I have only heard of ending without finishing; how can you finish by forcing an end?" Hsueh said, "The immense billows rise a thousand fathoms; the clear waves are not other than water." Ch'ing said, "When one phrase cuts off the flow, myriad impulses cease." Hsueh thereupon bowed. Ch'ing tapped him three times with his whisk and said, "Exceptional indeed. Now sit and have tea."

When Feng Hsueh first came to Nan Yuan, he entered the door without bowing. Yuan said, "When you enter the door, you should deal with the host." Hsueh said, "I ask the Teacher to make a definite distinction." Yuan slapped his knee with his left hand. Hsueh immediately shouted. Yuan slapped his knee with his right hand. Hsueh again shouted. Yuan raised his left hand and said, "This one I concede to you." Then he raised his right hand and said, "But what about this one?" Hsueh said, "Blind!" Yuan then raised his staff. Hsueh said, "What are you doing? I will take that staff away from you and hit you, Teacher; don't say I didn't warn you. Yuan then threw the staff down and said, "Today I have been made a fool of by this yellow-faced riverlander." Hsueh said, "Teacher, it seems you are unable to hold your bowl, yet are falsely claiming you're not hungry." Yuan said, "Haven't you ever reached this place?" Hsueh said, "What kind of talk is this?" Yuan said, "I just asked." Hsueh said, "Still I can't let you go." Yuan said, "Sit awhile and drink some tea."

See how an excellent student naturally has a sharp and dangerous edge to his personality. Even Nan Yuan couldn't really handle him. The next day, Nan Yuan just posed an ordinary question, saying "Where did you spend this summer?" Hsueh said, "I passed the summer along with Attendant Kuo at the Deer Gate." Yuan said, "So really you had already personally seen an adept when you came here." Yuan also said, "What did he say to you?" Hsueh said, "From beginning to end he only taught me to always be the master." Yuan immediately struck him and drove him out of the abbot's room; he said, "What is the use of a man who accepts defeat?"

Hsueh henceforth submitted. In Nan Yuan's community he worked as the gardener. One day Nan Yuan came to the garden and questioned him; he said, "How do they bargain for the staff in the South?" Hsueh said, "They make a special bargain. How do they bargain for it here, Teacher?" Nan Yuan raised his staff and said, "Under the staff, acceptance of birthlessness; facing the situation without deferring to the teacher." At this Feng Hsueh opened up in great enlightenment.

At this time the five dynasties were divided and at war. The governor of Ying Chou invited the Master (Feng Hsueh) to pass the summer there. At this time the one school of Lin Chi greatly flourished. Whenever he questioned and answered, or gave out pointers, invariably his words were sharp and fresh; gathering flowers, forming brocade, each word had a point.

One day the governor requested the Master to enter the hall to teach the assembly. The Master said, "The Patriarchal Teacher's Mind Seal is formed like the workings of the Iron Ox. Removed, the impression remains; left, the impression is ruined. But if you neither take it away nor keep it there, is it right to use the seal or not?"

Why is it not like the workings of a stone man or a wooden horse, only like the workings of an Iron Ox? There is no way for you to move it: wherever you go the seal remains; as soon as you stop, the seal is broken, causing you to shatter into a hundred fragments. But if you neither go nor stay, should you use the seal or not? See how he gives out indications; you might say there is bait on the hook.

At this time there was an Elder Lu P'i in the audience. He also was a venerable adept in the tradition of Lin Chi. He dared to come forth and reply to his device; thus he turned his words and made a question, undeniably unique; "I have the workings of an Iron Ox; I ask you, Master, not to impress the seal." But what could he do? Feng Hsueh was an adept; he immediately replied to him, saying, "Accustomed to scouring the oceans fishing for whales, I regret to find instead a frog crawling in the muddy river sand." And there is an echo in the words. Yun Men said, "Trailing a hook in the four seas, just fishing for a hideous dragon; the mysterious device beyond convention is to seek out those who understand the self."

In the vast ocean, twelve buffalo carcasses are used as bait for the hooks; instead he has just snagged a frog. But there is nothing mysterious or wonderful in these words; and neither is there any principle to judge. An Ancient said, "It is easy to see in the phenomenon: if you try to figure it out in your mind, you will lose contact with it." Lu P'i stood there thinking: "Seeing it, if you don't take it, it will be hard to find again even in a

thousand years." What a pity! That is why it is said, "Even if
you can explain a thousand scriptures and commentaries, it is
hard to utter a phrase appropriate to the moment."

The fact is that Lu P'i was searching for a good saying to
answer Feng Hsueh; he didn't want to carry out the order, and
suffered Feng Hsueh's thoroughgoing use of his ability to "capture the flag and steal the drum." He was unremittingly
pressed back, and simply couldn't do anything. As a proverb
says, "When an army is defeated, it cannot be swept up with a
grass broom." In the very beginning it is still necessary to seek
a tactic to oppose the adversary, but if you wait till you've
come up with one, your head will have fallen to the ground.

The governor too had studied a long time with Feng Hsueh;
he knew to say, "The Law of Buddhas and the Law of Kings are
one." Hsueh said, "What have you seen?" The governor said,
"If you do not settle what should be settled, instead you bring
on disorder." Feng Hsueh was all one whole mass of spirit, like
a gourd floating on the water; press it down and it rolls over;
push it and it moves. He knew how to explain the Dharma
according to the situation; if it did not accord with the situation, it would just be false talk. Hsueh thereupon left the seat.

VERSE

Having caught Lu P'i, he makes him mount the Iron Ox:
> Among a thousand people, ten thousand, still he wants to
> show his skill. The general of a defeated army need not be
> decapitated a second time.

The spear and armor of the Three Profundities have never been
> *easily opposed;*
> The one whose move it is, is confused. He accepts disaster
> like receiving good fortune and accepts submission like
> encountering opposition.

By the castle of the King of Ch'u, the tidal water—
> What tidal water are you talking about? Vastly extensive,
> it fills heaven and earth. Even were it the four seas, he
> would still reverse their flow.

Shouting once he caused its flow to turn back.
　　This one shout not only cuts off your tongue; oh! it star-
　　tles the Iron Ox of Shensi into a run and frightens the
　　Great Colossus of Chia Chou[b] to death.

COMMENTARY

Hsueh Tou knew Feng Hsueh to have such a style, so he
eulogized him by saying, "Having caught Lu P'i, he mounts
him on the Iron Ox; the spear and armor of the three profundities have never been easily opposed." In the tradition of Lin
Chi there are three profundities and three essentials: within
any one phrase there must be inherent three profundities; in
one profundity there must be inherent three essentials. A
monk asked Lin Chi, "What is the primary phrase?" Chi said,

　　When the seal of the three essentials is lifted, the
　　　red mark is narrow;
　　Without admitting hesitation, host and guest are
　　　distinct.

"What is the secondary phrase?"

　　How can subtle discernment admit of no question-
　　　ing?
　　Expedients do not go against the ability to cut off
　　　the streams.

"What is the third phrase?"

　　Just observe the playing of puppets on the stage:
　　The pulling of the strings depends on the man be-
　　　hind the scenes.

In Feng Hsueh's one phrase, he is immediately equipped with
the spear and armor of the three profundities; with seven accoutrements[c] at his side, it is not easy to oppose him. If he were
not so, how could he have handled Lu P'i?
　　Finally, Hsueh Tou wants to bring out the active edge of the
Lin Chi line: do not speak only of Lu P'i—even by the castle of
the King of Ch'u, the great waves, vast and extensive, the white
breakers flooding the sky, all return to the source; just using a
single shout is all that's needed to make them reverse their
course.

TRANSLATORS' NOTES

a. The Iron Ox is supposed to have been built by the legendary King Yu to stem the flood of the Yellow River some four thousand years ago; its head is in Honan, and its tail is in Hopei.
b. A huge stone image of Maitreya, said to be three hundred sixty feet high.
c. The seven items that make up the teacher's accoutrements: 1) great capacity and great function; 2) swiftness of wit and eloquence; 3) wondrous spirituality of speech; 4) the active edge to kill or bring to life; 5) wide learning and broad experience; 6) clarity of mirroring awareness; 7) freedom to appear or disappear. "The seven accoutrements" can also refer to a warrior's set of equipment.

Yun Men's Flowering Hedge

POINTER

One who can take action on the road is like a tiger in the mountains; one immersed in worldly understanding is like a monkey in a cage. If you want to know the meaning of buddha-nature, you should observe times and seasons, causes and conditions. If you want to smelt pure gold which has been refined a hundred times, you need the forge and bellows of a master. Now tell me, when one's great function appears, what can be used to test him?

CASE

A monk asked Yun Men, "What is the Pure Body of Reality?"[1]

Yun Men said, "A flowering hedge."[2]

The monk asked, "What is it like when one goes on in just such a way?"[3]

Yun Men said, "A golden-haired lion."[4a]

NOTES

1. He sees the sixteen-foot golden body (of Buddha) in a heap of dust. Mottled and mixed up; what is it?
2. If the point of the question is not real, the answer comes across crude. Striking, resounding (everywhere). The bent does not hide the straight.
3. He swallows the date whole. Why indulge in stupidity?
4. He is both praising and censuring; two faces of one die. He adds error to error—what is going on in his mind?

COMMENTARY

People, do you know the point of this monk's questions and the point of Yun Men's answers? If you do know, their two mouths are alike without a single tongue. If you do not know, you will not avoid being fatheaded.

A monk asked Hsuan Sha, "What is the Pure Body of Reality?" Sha said, "Dripping with pus." He had the adamantine eye: as a test, I ask you to try to discern it.

Yun Men was not the same as others. Sometimes he held still and stood like a wall ten miles high, with no place for you to draw near. Sometimes he would open out a path for you, die along with you and live along with you.

Yun Men's tongue was very subtle; some people say he was answering him figuratively; but if you understand it this way, then tell me where Yun Men is at. This was a household affair; do not try to figure it out from outside. This was the reason Pai Chang said, "Manifold appearances and myriad forms, and all spoken words, each should be turned and returned to oneself and made to turn freely." Going to where life springs forth, he immediately speaks; if you try to discuss it and seek it in thought, immediately you have fallen into the secondary phase. Yung Chia said, "When the Body of Reality awakens fully, there is not a single thing; the inherent nature of the original source is the natural real Buddha."

Yun Men tested this monk; the monk was also a member of his household and was himself a longtime student. He knew the business of the household, so he went on to say, "What is it like to go on like this?"Men said, "A golden-haired lion." But tell me, is this agreeing with him or not agreeing with him? Is this praising him or censuring him? Yen T'ou said, "If you engage in a battle, each individual stands in a pivotal position." It is also said, "He studies the living phrase; he does not study the dead phrase. If you get understanding at the living phrase, you will never ever forget; if you get understanding at the dead phrase, you will be unable to save yourself."

Another monk asked Yun Men, "Is it true or not that 'the Buddha Dharma is like the moon in the water'?" Yun Men said, "There is no way through the clear waves." The monk went on to say, "How did you manage?" Yun Men said,

"Where does this second question come from?" The monk said, "How is it when going on in just this way?" Yun Men said, "Further complications block the mountain path."

You must realize that this matter does not rest in words and phrases: like sparks from struck flint, like the brilliance of flashing lightning, whether you reach it or not, you still will not avoid losing your body and life. Hsueh Tou is someone who is there: so he produces his verse from that very place.

VERSE

A flowering hedge:
   The words are still in our ears.
Don't be fatheaded!
   Such people are numerous as hemp and millet seeds. Still, there are some who are not.
The marks are on the balance arm, not on the scale pan.
   Too complicated! Everyone should go to his own place and introspect. He hasn't avoided talking about principle.
"So just be like this"—
   He swallows the date whole.
How pointless!
   Take what's yours and get out. Clearly. You should not mistakenly blame Yun Men.
A golden-haired lion—everybody look!
   He lets out one or a half. Still they are dogs. Yun Men is also a man from P'u Chou escorting a thief.

COMMENTARY

Hsueh Tou sizes up the audience to give his order; he makes the harpstring move and distinguishes the tune. With each phrase he continues the judgement. This one verse is not at variance with the form for quoting the Ancients: "A flowering hedge"; then he says, "Don't be fatheaded." People all say that Yun Men was responding figuratively; they all make up emotional interpretations to understand him. Hsueh Tou therefore gives his own fodder and says, "Don't be fatheaded." All in all, Yun Men's meaning does not lie where the flowering hedge is; that is why Hsueh Tou says, "The marks are on the balance arm, not on the scale pan." This one phrase is excessively indulgent. In the water there is originally no moon; the moon is in the sky. This is like the marks being on the balance arm, not on the scale pan. But tell me, which is the balance? If you can discern it clearly, you will not turn away from Hsueh Tou.

When that man of old got to this point, he was undeniably compassionate. Clearly he says to you, "It's not here; it's over there." But tell me, what place is that "over there"? This finishes the eulogizing of their first statements; afterwards he versifies the monk's saying, "What is it like when just going on like this?" Hsueh Tou says that this monk still has no point. But tell me, is this meeting in the light or meeting in darkness? Did he speak this way from understanding, or did he speak thus without understanding? "A golden-haired lion—everyone look!" Do you see the golden-haired lion? Look!

TRANSLATORS' NOTES

a. The Golden-haired Lion is used in the Hua Yen school to symbolize the cosmos as the mutual interpenetration of the universal and the particular, of principle (relativity, emptiness of inherent fixed reality) and phenomena (the myriads of things and events). The Lion's whole body is reflected in each and every hair: thus there is an infinity of infinities within the whole, with each particular hair reflected in and reflecting the others ad infinitum. In a general way the Golden-haired Lion represents reality, or the embodiment of reality. Manjusri, the bodhisattva who stands for wisdom and knowledge, is depicted as riding the Golden-haired Lion.

Nan Ch'uan's It's like a Dream

POINTER

Cease and desist; then an iron tree blooms with flowers. Is there anyone? Is there? A clever lad loses his profits; even though he is free in seven ways up and down and eight ways across, he cannot avoid having another pierce his nostrils. But tell me, where is his error? To test, I quote this to see.

CASE

As the officer Lu Hsuan was talking with Nan Ch'uan, he said, "Master of the Teachings Chao said, 'Heaven, earth, and I have the same root; myriad things and I are one body.' This is quite marvelous."[1]

Nan Ch'uan pointed to a flower in the garden.[2] He called to the officer and said, "People these days see this flower as a dream."[3]

NOTES

1. He's making a living in a ghost cave. A picture of a cake cannot satisfy hunger. This is also haggling in the weeds.
2. What is he saying? Bah! The scriptures have teachers of scriptures, the treatises have teachers of treatises: it's no business of a patchrobed monk. Bah! A powerful man in that instance would have uttered a turning word, and not only cut off Nan Ch'uan, but thereby cause all the patchrobed monks to show some energy.
3. When the mandarin duck embroidery is done, you may look at them, but do not give the golden needle away to anyone. Don't talk in your sleep! You have drawn the golden oriole down from his willow branch.

COMMENTARY

The officer Lu Hsuan studied for a long time with Nan Ch'uan. He always kept his mind on essential nature, and he immersed himself in the *Discourses of Chao*. One day as they sat, he happened to bring up these two lines, considering them remarkable. He questioned, "Master of the Teachings Chao said, 'Heaven, earth, and I have the same root; myriad things and I are one body.' This is quite marvelous." Master of the Teachings Seng Chao was an eminent monk of Chin times (latter 4th–early 5th centuries A.D.); he was together with Tao Sheng, Tao Jung, and Seng Jui in the school of Kumarajiva. They were called the Four Sages.

When (Seng Chao) was young, he enjoyed reading Chuang Tzu and Lao Tzu. Later, as he was copying the old translation of the Vimalakirti Scripture, he had an enlightenment. Then he knew that Chuang and Lao still were not really thoroughgoing. Therefore he compiled all the scriptures and composed four discourses.

What Chuang and Lao intended to say was that "heaven and earth are greatness of form; my form is also thus; we are alike born in the midst of empty nothingness." Chuang and Lao's overall meaning just discusses equalizing things; Seng Chao's overall meaning says that nature all returns to self. Have you not seen how his discourse says, "The ultimate man is empty and hollow, without form; yet none of the myriad things are not his own doing. Who can understand that myriad things are his own self? Only a sage, I wot."

Although there are spirits and there are humans, there are the wise and the sage, each is distinct, but all alike have one nature and one substance.

An Ancient said, "Heaven and earth, the whole world, is just one self; when cold, it is cold throughout heaven and earth; when hot, it is hot throughout heaven and earth. When it exists, all throughout heaven and earth exists; when it doesn't exist, heaven and earth do not exist. When affirmed, all throughout heaven and earth is; when denied, all throughout heaven and earth is not."

Fa Yen said,

He he he I I I
South north east west, everything is all right.
All right or not all right,
Only for me there is nothing not all right.

That is why it was said, "In the heavens and on earth, only I alone am honorable." As Shih T'ou read the *Discourse of Chao,* when he got to this place, "Understand myriad things as oneself," he was vastly and greatly enlightened. Later he composed the book *Ts'an T'ung Ch'i* ("Merging of Difference and Sameness"), which also does not go beyond this meaning.

See how (Lu Hsuan) questioned; tell me, what root do they share? Which body do they have in common? When he got here, still he was undeniably unique: how could this be the same as an ordinary man's ignorance of the height of the sky or the breadth of the earth? How could there be such a thing?

Lu Hsuan's questioning in this manner was indeed quite exceptional, but he did not go beyond the meaning of the Teachings. If you say that the meaning of the Teachings is the ultimate paradigm, then why did the World Honored One also raise the flower?[a] What did the Patriarchal Teacher come from the West for?

Nan Ch'uan's way of answering used the grip of a patch-robed monk to pull out the painful spot for the other, and broke up his nest; he pointed at a flower in the garden and called to the officer, saying, "People these days see this flower as though it were a dream." This is like leading the man to the edge of a ten thousand fathom cliff and giving him a push, causing his life to be cut off. If you were pushed over on level ground, even till Maitreya Buddha was born in the world, you still would simply be unable to accomplish the cutting off of life.

It is also like a man in a dream; though he wants to awaken, he cannot wake up; called by another, he awakens. If Nan Ch'uan's eyes were not true, he would certainly have been befuddled by Lu. See how he talks; yet undeniably he is difficult to understand. If the action of your eyes is alive, you will experience it like the superb flavor of ghee; if you are dead, you will hear it and turn it into poison. An Ancient said, "If you see it in phenomena, you'll fall into ordinary feelings; if you go to your intellect to figure it out, after all you will seek without finding." Yen T'ou said, "This is the livelihood of a transcendent man; he just reveals the bit before the eyes, just like a flash of lightning."

Nan Ch'uan's great meaning was like this; he has the capability to capture rhinos and tigers, to judge dragons and snakes. When you get here, you must understand on your own: have you not heard it said, "The single transcending road has not been transmitted by a thousand sages; students toil over forms like moneys grasping at reflections." See how Hsueh Tou brings it out in verse:

VERSE

Seeing, hearing, awareness, knowledge; these are not one and
*   the same—*
  In the multitude of forms and myriad appearances, there is not a single thing. Seven flowers, eight blooms.[b] Eye, ear, nose, tongue, body and mind are all at once a hammerhead without a hole.

Mountains and rivers are not seen in a mirror.
  There is no such scenery here where I am. What is long is of itself long; what is short is of itself short; green is green and yellow is yellow. Where do you see them?

The frosty sky's moon sets, the night nearly half over;
  He has led you into the weeds. The whole world has never concealed it. I only fear you will go sit inside a ghost cave.

With whom will it cast a shadow, cold in the clear pool?
  Is there anyone? Is there? If they did not sleep on the same bed, how could they know the cover is worn out? Someone who is sad should not speak of it to another who is sad; if he speaks to a sad man, it would sadden him to death.

COMMENTARY

Nan Ch'uan's little sleep talk, Hsueh Tou's big sleep talk: although they are dreaming, they are having a good dream. At first there was talk of 'one body'—here he says that they are not the same: "Seeing, hearing, awareness, and knowledge are not one and the same— / Mountains and rivers are not seen in a mirror." If you say that they are seen in a mirror, and only then illumined, then they are not apart from where the mirror is. Mountains, rivers, and the great earth; plants, trees, and forests —do not use a mirror to observe them. If you use a mirror to observe, then you make it into two parts. Just let mountains be mountains and rivers be rivers. "Each thing abides in its normal state; the mundane aspect always remains."

"Mountains and rivers are not seen in a mirror." Then tell me, where can you see them? Do you understand? When you get here, turn towards: "The frosty sky's moon sets, the night nearly half over"—This Side he has summed up for you; That Side, you must cross by yourself.

But do you realize that Hsueh Tou uses his own thing to help others? "With whom will it cast a shadow, cold in the clear pool?" Do you think he is reflected himself, or do you think he is reflected together with anyone?[c] It is necessary to cut off mental activity and cut off understanding before finally reaching this realm.

Right now, we don't need a clear pool, and we don't have to wait for the moon to set in the frosty sky. Right now, how is it?

TRANSLATORS' NOTES

a. This incident marks the beginning of the 'separate transmission' of Ch'an: at the assembly on Vulture Peak, the Buddha raised a flower. No one in the crowd understood his meaning but Mahakasyapa, who gave a slight smile. Thus Buddha recognized Mahakasyapa as the heir to the treasury of the eye of the true teaching.

b. 'Seven flowers, eight blooms' is one literal translation of a phrase that bears multiple meanings. It can mean profusion, confusion in multiplicity, 'cracked and shattered.' It can also mean opened up, clearly distinct, everything revealed in all its multiplicity.

c. According to the *Shudensho*, the moon's setting can be interpreted as 'descending,' or shining into the pool, casting a reflection: is it just the moon alone, or is anyone there? The ambiguity of the subject makes this passage difficult to translate, while the ambivalence itself underscores the unity of self and world.

Chao Chou's Man Who Has Died the Great Death

POINTER

Where right and wrong are mixed, even the sages cannot know; when going against and with, vertically and horizontally, even the Buddhas cannot know. One who is a man detached from the world, who transcends convention, reveals the abilities of a great man who stands out from the crowd. He walks on thin ice, runs on a sword's edge. He is like the unicorn's horn, like a lotus flower in fire. When he sees someone beyond comparison, he knows they are on the same path. Who is an expert? As a test I'm citing this old case: look!

CASE

Chao Chou asked T'ou Tzu, "How is it when a man who has died the great death returns to life?"[1]

T'ou Tzu said, "He must not go by night: he must get there in daylight."[2]

NOTES

1. There are such things! A thief doesn't strike a poor household. He is accustomed to acting as guest, thus he has a feel for guests.
2. Seeing a cage, he makes a cage. This is a thief recognizing a thief. If he wasn't lying on the same bed, how would he know the coverlet is worn?

COMMENTARY

Chao Chou asked T'ou Tzu, "How is it when a man who has died the great death returns to life?" T'ou Tzu answered him saying, "He must not go by night: he must get there in day-light." But say, what time and season is this? A flute with no holes strikes against a felt-pounding board. This is called "a question to test the host"; it is also called "an intentional question." All over they praised T'ou Tzu and Chao Chou for having outstanding eloquence. Though the two old men suc-ceeded to different masters, observe how their active edges accord as one.

One day T'ou Tzu spread the tea setting to entertain Chao Chou. T'ou Tzu himself passed some steamed cakes to Chao Chou, but Chou paid no attention. T'ou Tzu ordered his atten-dant to give the sesame cakes to Chao Chou. Chou bowed to the attendant three times. But say, what was his meaning? Observe how he always went right to the root to uphold this fundamental thing for the benefit of others.

There was a monk who asked T'ou Tzu, "What is the Way?" T'ou Tzu answered, "The Way." The monk asked, "What is Buddha?" T'ou Tzu answered, "Buddha." Again he asked, "How is it before the golden lock is open?" T'ou Tzu answered, "Open." He asked, "How is it before the golden rooster has crowed?" T'ou Tzu answered, "This sound does not exist." The monk asked, "How is it after he crows?" T'ou Tzu an-swered, "Each knows the time for himself." His whole life T'ou Tzu's questions and answers were all like this.

Look: when Chao Chou asked, "How is it when a man who has died the great death returns to life?" T'ou Tzu immediately said, "He must not go by night: he must get there in daylight." Direct as sparks struck from stone, like the brilliance of a lightning flash. Only a transcendental man like him could do this.

A man who has died the great death has no Buddhist doc-trines and theories, no mysteries and marvels, no gain and loss, no right and wrong, no long and short. When he gets here, he just lets it rest this way. An Ancient said of this, "On the level ground the dead are countless; only one who can pass through the forest of thorns is a good hand." Yet one must pass beyond that Other Side too to begin to attain. Even so, for present day people even to get to this realm is already difficult to achieve.

If you have any leanings or dependence, any interpretative understanding, then there is no connection. Master Che called this "vision that is not purified." My late teacher Wu Tsu called it "the root of life not cut off." One must die the great death once, then return to life. Master Yung Kuang of central Chekiang said, "If you miss at the point of their words, then you're a thousand miles from home. In fact you must let go your hands while hanging from a cliff, trust yourself and accept the experience. Afterwards you return to life again. I can't deceive you—how could anyone hide this extraordinary truth?"

The meaning of Chao Chou's question is like this. T'ou Tzu is an adept, and he didn't turn his back on what Chao Chou asked: it's just that he cut off his feelings and left no traces, so unavoidably he's hard to understand. He just showed the little bit before the eyes. Thus an Ancient said, "If you want to attain Intimacy, don't ask with questions. The question is in the answer, and the answer is in the question." It would have been very difficult for someone other than T'ou Tzu to reply when questioned by Chao Chou. But since T'ou Tzu is an expert, as soon as it's raised he knows where it comes down.

VERSE

In life there's an eye—still, it's the same as death.
  The two don't know of each other. Back and forth, coming and going. If Chao Chou wasn't well provided, how could he discern whether T'ou Tzu was monk or lay?

Why use antiserum to test an adept?
  If you don't test how can you discern the truth? Having met, try to give an examination—what's the harm? I too want to question him.

Even the Ancient Buddhas, they say, have never arrived.
  Luckily they had companions. Even the thousand sages haven't transmitted it. I don't know either.

I don't know who can scatter dust and sand.
  There is quite a bit of this right now. (The dust and sand) gets in your eyes whether they're opened or closed. When you bring it up this way, Your Reverence, where does it come down?

COMMENTARY

"In life there's an eye—still, it's the same as death." Hsueh Tou is a man who knows what is, therefore he can dare to make up verses. An Ancient said, "He studies the living phrase; he doesn't study the dead phrase." Hsueh Tou says that to have eyes within life is still to be just the same as a dead man. Has he ever died? To have eyes within death is to be the same as a live man. An Ancient said, "Utterly kill a dead man, then you will see a live man. Bring a dead man fully to life, then you will see a dead man."

Though Chao Chou is a live man, he intentionally made up a dead question to test T'ou Tzu. It was like taking a substance that vitiates the character of a medicine in order to test him. That's why Hsueh Tou said, "Why use antiserum to test an adept?" This versifies Chao Chou's questioning.

Afterwards he praises T'ou Tzu: "Even the Ancient Buddhas, they say, have never arrived." Even the ancient Buddhas never got to where the man who has died the great death returns to life—nor have the venerable old teachers ever gotten here. Even old Shakyamuni or the blue-eyed barbarian monk (Bodhidharma) would have to study again before they get it. That is why Hsueh Tou said, "I only grant that the old barbarian knows; I don't allow that he understands."

Hsueh Tou says, "I don't know who can scatter dust and sand." Haven't you heard: a monk asked Ch'ang Ch'ing, "What is the eye of a man of knowledge?" Ch'ing said, "He has a vow not to scatter sand." Pao Fu said, "You mustn't scatter any more of it." All over the country venerable old teachers sit on carved wood seats, using blows and shouts, raising their whisks, knocking on the seat, exhibiting spiritual powers and acting as masters—all of this is scattering sand. But say, how can this be avoided?

Layman P'ang's Good Snowflakes

POINTER

Bringing it out unique and alone (is still) dripping with water, dragging through mud. When knocking and resounding occur together (it's still like) a silver mountain, an iron wall.

If you describe and discuss, you see ghosts in front of your skull. If you seek in thought, you sit beneath the black mountain. The bright shining sun lights up the sky. The pure whispering wind circles the earth.

But say, do the Ancients have any obscurities? To test I'm citing this old case: look!

CASE

When Layman P'ang took leave of Yao Shan[1], Shan ordered ten Ch'an travellers to escort him to the gate.[2] The Layman pointed to the snow in the air and said, "Good snowflakes—they don't fall in any other place."[3]

At the time one of the Ch'an travellers named Ch'uan said, "Where do they fall?"[4] The Layman slapped him once.[5] Ch'uan said, "Even a layman shouldn't be so coarse."[6] The Layman said, "Though you call yourself a Ch'an traveller this way, the King of Death still won't let you go."[7] Ch'uan said, "How about you, Layman?"[8] Again the Layman slapped him[9] and said, "Your eyes see like a blind man, your mouth speaks like a mute."[10]

Hsueh Tou said besides, "When P'ang first spoke I just would have made a snowball and hit him with it."[11]

NOTES

1. This old fellow is acting strange.
2. Yao Shan does not take him lightly. What realm is this? Only a

patchrobed monk who knows the whole thing could (give P'ang this treatment).

3. He stirs up waves where there's no wind. The finger (he points with) has eyes. There's an echo in this old fellow's words.

4. On target. He comes on following after P'ang. Of course he climbed onto P'ang's hook.

5. A hit! As it turns out, the thief that Ch'uan pulled in ransacked his house.

6. Staring eyes inside a coffin.

7. The second ladleful of foul water has been poured over him. Why only the King of Death? Here I wouldn't let him go either.

8. His coarse mind hasn't changed. Again he's asking for a beating. From beginning to end this monk is at a loss.

9. Of course. Adding frost on top of snow. Having taken a beating, reveal the truth.

10. He has another conciliatory statement. Again he reads the verdict for him.

11. Hsueh Tou is right, but he draws the bow after the thief has gone. This is still quite indulgent. Nevertheless, I'd like to see their arrowpoints meet. But what can we do?—Hsueh Tou has fallen into the ghost cave.

COMMENTARY

Layman P'ang called on Ma Tsu and Shih T'ou: at both places he had verses (to express his realization).

When he first saw Shih Tou he asked, "What man doesn't keep company with the myriad things?" Before he stopped talking, he had his mouth covered by Shih T'ou and had an awakening. He made up a verse saying,

> My everyday affairs are no different:
> Only I myself naturally harmonize.
> No place is grasped or rejected,
> Nowhere do I go for or against.
> Who considers crimson and purple honorable?
> The green mountains have not a speck of dust.
> Spiritual powers and their wondrous functioning—
> Hauling water and carrying firewood.

Later P'ang called on Ma Tsu. Again he asked, "What man doesn't keep company with the myriad things?" Tsu said, "Wait till you can swallow all the water in West River in one gulp, then I'll tell you." The Layman emptied out in great enlightenment. He made up a verse saying,

> The ten directions, a common gathering—
> Everyone studies not-doing.
> This is the place where Buddhas are chosen—
> Minds empty, they return successful.

Since P'ang was an adept, all the various monasteries later welcomed him, and wherever he went they vied to praise him. After he had gotten to Yao Shan and stayed around there quite a while, he went to take leave of Yao Shan. Shan held him in the highest esteem, so he ordered ten Ch'an travellers to see him off. It happened to be snowing at the time: the Layman pointed to the snow and said, "Good snowflakes—they don't fall in any other place."

When Ch'an traveller Ch'uan asked, "Where do they fall?" the Layman immediately slapped him. Since Ch'uan was unable to carry out the order, the Layman ordered him to carry out half. Although the order was put into effect, when Ch'an traveller Ch'uan responded in this way, it was not that he didn't know what P'ang was getting at. They each had a point to their activity, but their rolling up and rolling out were not the same. Even so, in some respects he didn't come up to the Layman. That is why he fell into his trap and found it difficult to get out of the Layman's range.

After the Layman had hit him, the Layman went on to explain the reason to him saying, "Your eyes see like a blind man, your mouth speaks like a mute." Besides the previous words Hsueh Tou said, "When he first spoke I just would have made a snowball and hit him with it." Hsueh Tou talked this way, not wanting to turn his back on the question: it's just that his action was tardy. Librarian Ch'ing said, "The Layman's mind is like a lightning bolt. If we waited for you to grab a snowball, how long would it take? Only if you hit him while he's still speaking can you cut him off completely."

Hsueh Tou versifies his own hitting and says:

VERSE

The snowball hits! The snowball hits!
> What will he do about falling into a secondary action? It's
> not worth the trouble to bring it forth. Overhead vastness,
> underfoot vastness.

Old Pang's ability cannot grasp it.
> Again and again there are people who don't know this. I
> only fear it's not so.

Gods and humans do not know for themselves:
> What scene is this? Does Hsueh Tou know?

In eyes, in ears, absolutely clean.
> The arrowpoints meet. Your eyes see like a blind man,
> your mouth speaks like a mute.

Absolutely clean—
> How? Where will you see Layman P'ang and Hsueh Tou?

Even the blue-eyed barbarian monk Bodhidharma would find
> *it hard to discriminate.*
> Bodhidharma comes forth: what does he say to you? I'll
> hit saying, "What are you saying?" They're buried in the
> same pit.

COMMENTARY

"The snowball hits! The snowball hits! / Old P'ang's ability
cannot grasp it." Hsueh Tou wanted to walk on the Layman's
head. The Ancients used "snow" to illustrate the matter of
Uniformity. Hsueh Tou meant: "If at that time I had made a
snowball and hit him with it, no matter what abilities the
Layman had, it would have been hard for him to reach (me.)"
Hsueh Tou praises his own hitting, far from knowing where
he's lost his profit.

"Gods and men do not know for themselves: / In eyes, in
ears, absolutely clean." In the eyes is snow, in the ears is snow
too—just at that moment they are dwelling in Uniformity.
This is also called "the realm of Samantabhadra." The
phenomenon of Uniformity is also called "becoming solid."

Yun Men said, "Even 'having not the slightest worry in the world' is still a turning phrase." When you don't see a single form, this finally is half the issue. If you want the whole issue, first you must know that there is a single road going beyond; when you get here your great function must become manifest (with no gap) for even a needle to enter, and you don't accept the judgments of other people.

Thus it was said, "He studies the living phrase; he doesn't study the dead phrase." An Ancient said, "An appropriate statement is a stake at which to tether a donkey for ten thousand eons." What's the use?

When he gets to this point Hsueh Tou has finished the verse. But he turns around again and says, "But this cleanness is absolute—even Bodhidharma would find it hard to discriminate." Since even Bodhidharma finds it hard to discern, what more would you have me say?

Tung Shan's No Cold or Heat

POINTER

Ten thousand ages abide by the phrase that determines heaven and earth. Even the thousand sages cannot judge the ability to capture tigers and rhinos. Without any further traces of obstruction, the whole being appears everywhere equally.

If you want to understand the hammer and tongs of transcendence, you need the forge and bellows of an adept.

But say, since ancient times has there ever been such a family style or not? To test I'm citing this old case: look!

CASE

A monk asked Tung Shan, "When cold and heat come, how can we avoid them?"[1]

Shan said, "Why don't you go to the place where there is no cold or heat?"[2]

The monk said, "What is the place where there is no cold or heat?"[3]

Tung Shan said, "When it's cold, the cold kills you; when it's hot, the heat kills you."[4]

NOTES

1. It's not this season. (Cold and heat) are right in your face, right on your head. Where are you?
2. The world's people can't find it. He hides his body but reveals a shadow. A con man sells a bogus city of silver.
3. Tung Shan swindles everyone utterly. The monk turns around following him. As soon as Tung Shan lets down his hook the monk climbs onto it.
4. The real does not conceal the false, the crooked does not hide the straight. Looking out over the cliff he sees tigers and rhinos—this

is indeed an occasion to be sad. Tung Shan overturns the great ocean and kicks over Mt. Sumeru. But say, where is Tung Shan?

COMMENTARY

Master Hsin of Huang Lung picked this out and said, "Tung Shan puts the collar on the sleeve and cuts off the shirtfront under the armpits. But what could he do?—This monk didn't like it." Right then a monk came forward and asked Huang Lung, "How are they to be dealt with?" After a long silence Huang Lung said, "Peaceful meditation does not require mountains and rivers: when you have extinguished the mind, fire itself is cool."

Tell me all of you, where is Tung Shan's trap at? If you can clearly discern this, for the first time you will know how the five positions of the Tung Shan tradition of interchanging correct and biased[a] handle people in an extraordinary way. When you reach this transcendental realm, then you'll be able to be like this without needing any arrangements, and you'll spontaneously accord perfectly.

Thus it is said:

> *The biased within the correct:*
> *In the middle of the first night, before the moon shines,*
> *No wonder, when they meet, they don't recognize each other:*
> *Each is hidden, still embracing the aversion of former days.*
>
> *The correct within the biased:*
> *At dawn an old woman encounters an ancient mirror;*
> *Clearly she sees her face—there is no other reality.*
> *Don't go on mistaking the image for the head.*
>
> *Coming from within the correct:*
> *Within nothingness there's a road out of the dust.*
> *If you can just avoid violating the present taboo name,*
> *You'll still surpass the eloquent ones of former dynasties who silenced every tongue.*

Arrival within the biased:
When two swords cross points, there's no need to
  withdraw.
A good hand is like a lotus in fire—
Clearly he naturally has the energy to reach the
  heavens.

Arrival within both at once:
He does not fall into being or non-being—who dares
  to associate with him!
Everyone wants to get out of the ordinary flow,
But after all he returns and sits in the ashes.

Jurist Yuan of Fu Shan considers this case as being in the pattern of the five positions. If you understand one, then the rest are naturally easy to understand. Yen T'ou said, "It's like a gourd (floating) on the water: push it, and it rolls over without making any effort at all."

Once there was a monk who asked Tung Shan, "How is it when Manjusri and Samantabhadra come to call?" Shan said, "I'd drive them into a herd of water buffalo." The monk said, "Teacher, you enter hell fast as an arrow." Shan said, "I've got all their strength."

When Tung Shan said, "Why don't you go to the place where there is no cold or heat?" this was the correct within the biased. When the monk said, "What is the place where there is no cold or heat?" and Shan said, "When it's cold the cold kills you; when it's hot the heat kills you," this was the biased within the correct. Though it's correct, still it's biased; though it's biased, nevertheless it's complete. This is recorded in full detail in the Records of the Ts'ao Tung School. Had it been the Lin Chi tradition, there wouldn't have been so many things. With this kind of public case you must understand directly as soon as it is uttered.

Some say, "I like no cold no heat very much." What grasp do they have on the case? An Ancient said, "If you run on a sword's edge, you're fast. If you see with emotional consciousness, then you're slow."

Haven't you heard: A monk asked Ts'ui Wei, "What is the meaning of the Patriarch coming from the West?" Wei said, "When no one comes, I'll tell you," then went into the garden. The monk said, "There's no one right here: please, Teacher, tell me." Wei pointed to the bamboo and said, "This stalk is so tall, that stalk is so short." Suddenly the monk was greatly enlightened.

Again: Ts'ao Shan asked a monk, "When it's so hot, where will you go to avoid it?" The monk said, "I'll avoid it inside a boiling cauldron, within the coals of a furnace." Ts'ao Shan said, "How can it be avoided in a boiling cauldron or among the coals of a furnace?" The monk said, "The multitude of sufferings cannot reach there." See how the people of the Ts'ao Tung house naturally understood the conversation of people of their house.

Hsueh Tou uses the affairs of their house to produce his verse:

VERSE

He lets down his hand, but still it's the same as a ten
thousand fathom cliff:
Who can discern this without being an adept? Where are correct and biased not perfectly merged? Once the imperial edict is on its way the nobles get out of the road (to let it pass).

Why must correct and biased be in an arrangement?
If you do arrange them, where will you have Today? How will you not become involved in dualism? When the wind moves, the grasses bend down; where the water runs, streams form.

The ancient crystal palace reflects the bright moon,
Round and full. Just don't grasp the reflection, and don't run right in.

The sly hound of Han vainly runs up the stairs.
It isn't just this time. He's stumbled past. Why is he running after dirt? I'll hit and say you are a fellow student of this monk.

COMMENTARY

In the Ts'ao Tung tradition there is appearing in the world and not appearing in the world; there is letting down a hand and not letting down a hand. If you don't appear in the world, your eyes gaze at cloudy skies. If you appear in the world, then your head and face are covered with ashes and dirt.

"Eyes gazing at cloudy skies" is "on top of a ten thousand fathom peak." "Head and face covered with ashes and dirt" refers to the business of letting down a hand. Sometimes "head and face covered with ashes and dirt" is "on top of a ten thousand fathom peak." Sometimes "on top of a ten thousand fathom peak" is "head and faces covered with ashes and dirt." In reality, going into inhabited areas to let down a hand and standing alone on a solitary peak are the same. Having returned to the source and comprehended nature, it is no different from discriminating intelligence. You must avoid understanding them as two parts.

Thus Hsueh Tou said, "He lets down his hand, but still it's the same as a ten thousand fathom cliff." There's simply no place for you to approach. "Why must correct and biased be in an arrangement?" When it comes time to function, they are naturally like this, they are not in any arrangement. This praises Tung Shan's answer.

Afterwards he said, "The ancient crystal palace reflects the bright moon / The sly hound of Han vainly runs up the stairs." This just versifies this monk running after Tung Shan's words. In the Ts'ao Tung tradition they have "the stone woman," "the wooden horse," "the bottomless basket," "the pearl that shines (of itself) at night," "the dead snake," and so on, eighteen kinds. Their general purpose is to illustrate the position of the correct.

When Tung Shan answered, "Why not go to where there is no cold or heat?" this was like the moon shining in the ancient crystal palace, seeming to have a round reflection. The monk asked, "What is the place where there is no cold or heat?" This is just like the hound of Han chasing a clod of dirt: he runs frantically up the stairs to catch the moon's reflection. Tung Shan said, "When it's cold, the cold kills you; when it's hot, the heat kills you." This monk was like the hound of Han running up the stairs but not seeing the image of the moon.

"The hound of Han" comes out of *Essays on the Warring States* where it says, "He was a swift black dog belonging to the Han clan. The rabbits in the mountains were clever; only he could catch these rabbits." Hsueh Tou draws on this to make a comparison for this monk.

What about all of you—do you know where Tung Shan helped people?

After a long silence, Yuan Wu said, "What rabbits are you looking for?"

TRANSLATORS' NOTES

a. 'Correct' symbolizes emptiness, nirvana; 'biased' symbolizes matter-energy, samsara. The intrinsic identity of emptiness and matter-energy, nirvana and samsara, and hence the complementary unity of wisdom and compassion, is basic to Mahayana, or Great Vehicle Buddhism.

Ho Shan's Knowing How to Beat the Drum

CASE

Ho Shan imparted some words saying, "Cultivating study is called 'learning.' Cutting off study is called 'nearness.'[1] Going beyond these two is to be considered real going beyond."[2]

A monk came forward and asked, "What is 'real going beyond'?"[3] Shan said, "Knowing how to beat the drum."[4]

Again he asked, "What is the real truth?"[5] Shan said, "Knowing how to beat the drum."[6]

Again he asked, "'Mind is Buddha'—I'm not asking about this. What is not mind and not Buddha?"[7] Shan said, "Knowing how to beat the drum."[8]

Again he asked, "When a transcendent man comes, how do you receive him?"[9] Shan said, "Knowing how to beat the drum."[10]

NOTES

1. The world's patchrobed monks can't leap clear of this. An iron hammerhead with no handle hole. An iron spike.
2. What are you doing with the one eye on your forehead?
3. What is he saying? I'd blot it out with a single brush stroke. There's an iron spike.
4. An iron spike. Iron brambles. Hard, hard.
5. What is he saying? A doubled case. There's another iron spike.
6. An iron spike. Iron brambles. Hard, hard.
7. What is he saying? This garbage heap! The three sections are not the same. There's another iron spike.
8. An iron spike. Iron brambles. Hard, hard.
9. What is he saying? This monk encounters a fourth ladleful of his foul water. There's another iron spike.
10. An iron spike. Iron brambles. Hard, hard. But say, what does this really mean? In the morning he goes to India, in the evening he returns to China.

COMMENTARY

Ho Shan imparted some words saying, "Cultivating study is called 'learning.' Cutting off study is called 'nearness.' Going beyond these two is to be considered real going beyond." The words of this case come from the *Jewel Treasure Treatise.* To study till there is nothing to study is called "cutting off study." Thus it is said, "Shallow learning, deep enlightenment; deep learning, no enlightenment." This is called "cutting off study." Yung Chia, who was enlightened in one night at Ts'ao Ch'i, said, "Years ago I accumulated learning, consulted the commentaries, and searched scriptures and treatises. Once one's cultivation of studies is completed and exhausted, he is called a non-doing, free man of the Path, beyond study. When he reaches the point of cutting off study, only then for the first time is he near to the Path. When he manages to go beyond these two (aspects of) study, this is called 'real going beyond.'"

The monk too was undeniably bright and quick, so he picked up on these words to question Ho Shan. Shan said, "Knowing how to beat the drum." This is what is called flavorless words, flavorless speech. If you want to understand this case, you must be a transcendent man. Only then will you see that these words have nothing to do with inherent nature, nor is there anything about them to discuss. Understand directly like the bottom falling out of a bucket: only this is where a patchrobed monk rests easy and begins to be able to accord with the meaning of the Patriarch coming from the West. Thus Yun Men said, "Hsueh Feng's rolling a ball, Ho Shan's beating the drum, the National Teacher's bowl of water, Chao Chou's 'Drink some tea,'—all these are indications of the absolute."

Again the monk asked, "What is the real truth?" Shan said, "Knowing how to beat the drum." In the real truth not one other thing is set up. As for the worldly truth, the myriad things are all present. That there is no duality to real and conventional is the highest meaning of the holy truths.

Again the monk asked, " 'Mind is Buddha'—I'm not asking about this. What is not mind and not Buddha?" Shan said, "Knowing how to beat the drum." "What's mind is Buddha" is easy to seek. But when you get to that which is not mind and not Buddha, it's hard and there are few people who arrive.

Again the monk asked, "When a transcendent man comes, how do you receive him?" Shan said, "Knowing how to beat the drum." A transcendent man is a man who has passed through, who is free, purified, and at ease.

All over they consider these four phases as a message from the source: they are called Ho Shan's four beating the drums. This is just like the following:

A monk asked Ching Ch'ing, "At the beginning of a new year, is there any Buddha Dharma or not?" Ch'ing said, "There is." The monk said, "What is the Buddha Dharma at the beginning of a new year?" Ch'ing said, "Initiate good fortune on new year's day and the myriad things are all renewed." The monk said, "I thank the Master for the answer." Ch'ing said, "Today I lost the advantage." He had six kinds of losses like this answer.

Again: A monk asked the great teacher Ching Kuo, "How is it when a crane perches upon a lone pine?" Kuo said, "Beneath its feet, an embarrassing situation." He also asked, "How is it when snow covers the thousand mountains?" Kuo said, "After the sun comes out, an embarrassing situation." Again the monk asked, "Where did the spirits who protect the Teaching go during the purge of 845?" Kuo said, "For the two guardians outside the triple gate, an embarrassing situation." All over, these are called Ching Kuo's three embarrassments.

Again: Pao Fu asked a monk, "What Buddha is the one in the temple?" The monk said, "Try to decide for sure, Teacher." Fu said, "It's old Shakyamuni." The monk said, "Better not deceive people." Fu said, "On the contrary, it's you who are deceiving me." Fu also asked the monk, "What's your name?" The monk said, "Hsien Tse." (which means "all wet") Fu said, "How is it when you encounter withering dryness?" The monk said, "Who is the withering dry one?" Fu said, "I am." The monk said, "Better not deceive people, Teacher." Fu said, "On the contrary, it's you who are deceiving me." Again Fu asked the monk, "What work do you do that you eat till you're so big?" The monk said, "You're not so small yourself, Teacher." Fu made a crouching gesture. The monk said, "Better not deceive people, Teacher." Fu said, "On the contrary, it's you who are deceiving me." Fu also asked the bath keeper, "How wide is that cauldron (you heat the water in)?" The bath keeper aid, "Please, Teacher, measure and see." Fu went through the motions of measuring. The bath keeper said, "Better not deceive people, Teacher." Fu said, "On the contrary, it's you who are deceiving me." All over they call this Pao Fu's four deceptions of people.

, This main case is also like Hsueh Feng's four tubs of lacquer:[a] all were masters of our ancient sect. Each produces profound and marvelous teachings and devices to receive people.

Afterwords Hsueh Tou draws out a single continuous line based on Yun Men's teachings to his assembly, and versifies this public case.

VERSE

One hauls rock;

In the heart of the realm the emperor commands. A leper drags along his companions. A transcendent man comes this way.

A second moves earth.

Outside the passes the general gives orders. Both have their crimes covered by the same indictment. Those with the same disease sympathize with each other.

To shoot the bolt requires a ten-ton crossbow.

Even if it's got a ten-ton pull, it still won't be able to penetrate. It should not be used against light opposition; how could it be used for a dead frog?

The old master of Elephant Bone Cliff (Hsueh Feng) rolled balls—

There's another man who has come this way. He had an iron hammer head with no handle hole. Who doesn't know?

How could this equal Ho Shan's "Knowing how to beat the drum"?

An iron spike. It takes this old fellow to understand. One son has attained intimately.

I report for you to know:

Even Hsueh Tou hasn't seen it in dreams. He's adding frost on top of snow. Do you know?

Don't be careless!

Again there's a bit of utter confusion.

The sweet is sweet, the bitter is bitter.

Thanks for the answer. Hsueh Tou wrongly adds a footnote: he should be given thirty blows. Has he ever taken a beating? As before, dark vastness. I'll hit!

COMMENTARY

One day Kuei Tsung gave the general call to labor (summoning everyone) to haul rock. Tsung asked the Duty Distributor where he was going. The Duty Distributor said, "I'm going to haul rock." Tsung said, "For now I'll let you haul rock, but don't move the tree in the middle."

Whenever a newcomer arrived (at his place) Mu P'ing would first order him to move three loads of earth. Mu P'ing had a verse which he showed to his assembly saying:

> East Mountain Road is narrow, West Mountain is
>   low:
> New comers must not refuse three loads of mud.
> Alas, you've been traversing the roads so long,
> It's so clear, but you don't recognize it and instead
>   get lost.

Later there was a monk who asked Mu P'ing, "I don't ask about what is included in the three loads. What about what's outside the three loads?" P'ing said, "The Iron Wheel Emperor commands in his realm." The monk was speechless, so P'ing hit him.

This is why Hsueh Tou said, "One hauls rock / A second moves earth."

"To shoot the bolt requires a ten-ton crossbow." Hsueh Tou uses the ten-ton pull crossbow to explain this case: he wants you to see how Ho Shan helped people. If it's a monstrous dragon or tiger or some other fierce beast, then you use this crossbow. If it's a tiny bird or a creature of little consequence, of course you mustn't use the crossbow lightly. Hence a ten-ton crossbow does not shoot its bolt for a rat.

"The old master of Elephant Bone Cliff rolled balls." That is: one day Hsueh Feng saw Hsuan Sha coming and rolled out three wooden balls together. Hsuan Sha made a smashing gesture. Hsueh Feng profoundly approved of him.

Although all of these stories are instances of the great functioning of their entire capacities, none equal's Ho Shan's "Knowing how to beat the drum." How direct this is—but it's hard to understand. Thus Hsueh Tou said, "How could this equal Ho Shan's 'Knowing how to beat the drum'?"

Again he feared that people would just make their living on the words without knowing their source, (and thus be) careless.

Therefore he said, "I report for you to know: don't be careless!" You too must really get to this realm before you can understand. If you don't want to carelessly confuse things, "The sweet is sweet, the bitter is bitter." Though Hsueh Tou picked it up and played with it like this, in the end he can't leap clear of Ho Shan either.

TRANSLATORS' NOTES

a. "Hsueh Feng's four tubs of lacquer" refers to some incidents between Hsueh Feng and T'ou Tzu, recorded in the *Record of the Transmission of the Lamp:*

Hsueh Feng was attending on T'ou Tzu, who pointed to a piece of rock in front of his hut and said to Hsueh Feng, "All the Buddhas of past, present, and future are right here." Feng said, "One must know that there is one who is not here." T'ou Tzu then returned to his hut to sit, saying, "You dull tub of lacquer!"

Feng followed T'ou Tzu to call on the hermit of Lung Yen. Feng asked, "Where does the road of Lung Yen go to?" T'ou Tzu took his staff and pointed before them. Feng said, "Does it go east or go west?" T'ou Tzu said, "You tub of lacquer!"

Another day Feng asked, "How is it when 'immediately completed with a single stroke'?" T'ou Tzu said, "It's not someone of unsettled temperament." Feng said, "How is it when not using a single stroke?" T'ou Tzu said, "You tub of lacquer!"

One day when T'ou Tzu was in his hut sitting, Feng asked, "Master, is there anyone who comes here to study or not?" T'ou Tzu took a hoe from under his bed and threw it down in front of him. Feng said, "If so, then I'll dig right here." T'ou Tzu said, "This tub of lacquer is not quick."

Chao Chou's Seven-Pound Cloth Shirt

POINTER

When he must speak, he speaks—in the whole world there is no match for him. When he should act, he acts—his whole capacity doesn't defer (to anyone). He is like sparks struck from stone, like the brilliance of a flash of lightning, like a raging fire fanned by the wind, like a rushing torrent crossing a sword edge. When he lifts up the hammer and tongs of transcendence, you won't avoid losing your point and having your tongue tied.

He lets out a single continuous road. To test I'm citing it: look!

CASE

A monk asked Chao Chou, "The myriad things return to one. Where does the one return to?"[1]

Chou said, "When I was in Ch'ing Chou I made a cloth shirt. It weighed seven pounds."[2]

NOTES

1. He's pressing this old fellow. Piled in mountains, heaped up in ranges. He should avoid going to the ghost cave to make his living.
2. After all Chou goes in all directions, drawing a net that fills the sky. But do you see Chao Chou? He has picked up the nostrils of patchrobed monks.

COMMENTARY

If you understand "going immediately at one stroke," then you've pierced the nostrils of the world's old teachers all at once, and they can't do a thing about you. Naturally where water goes, a channel forms. But if you vacillate and hesitate, the old monk Chao Chou is under your feet. The essential point of the Buddhist Teaching is not a matter of many words or verbose speech.

A monk asked Chao Chou, "The myriad things return to one. Where does the one return to?" Yet Chou answered him saying, "When I was in Ch'ing Chou I made a cloth shirt; it weighed seven pounds." If you go to the words to discriminate you are mistakenly abiding by the zero point of a scale. If you don't go to the words to discriminate, what can you do about it that he did nevertheless speak this way? This case, though hard to see, is nevertheless easy to understand; though easy to understand, it's still hard to see. Insofar as it's hard, it's a silver mountain, an iron wall. Insofar as it's easy, you are directly aware. There's no place for your calculations of right and wrong.

This story is the same kind as the story of P'u Hua saying, "Tomorrow there's a feast at the Temple of Great Compassion."[a]

One day a monk asked Chao Chou, "What is the meaning of the Patriarch coming from the West?" Chou said, "The cypress tree in the garden." The monk said, "Don't use objects to teach people with, Teacher." Chou said, "I've never used objects to teach people." Observe how, at the ultimate point, where it is impossible to turn, he does turn, and spontaneously covers heaven and earth. If you can't turn, wherever you set foot on the road you get stuck.

But say, did Chao Chou ever have discussions of Buddhist doctrine or not? If you say he did, when has he ever spoken of mind or of nature, of mysteries or of marvels? If you say he didn't have the source meaning of the Buddhist Teaching, when has he ever turned his back on anyone's question?

Haven't you heard: a monk asked Mu P'ing, "What is the great meaning of the Buddhist Teaching?" P'ing said, "This winter melon is so big." Again: a monk asked an ancient worthy, "Deep in the mountains on an overhanging cliff, in a remote, inaccessible, uninhabited place, is there any Buddhist Teaching or not?" The ancient worthy said, "There is." The monk said, "What is the Buddhist Teaching deep within the mountains?" The ancient worthy said, "The large rocks are large, the small ones small."

When you look at such a case, where are the obscurities? Hsueh Tou knows what they come down to: thus he opens up a road of meaning and comes out with a verse for you:

VERSE

He wraps everything up and presses against the ancient old awl.
    What's the need to press this old fellow? They push and push back—to where?
How many people know the weight of the seven-pound shirt?
    To bring it out again is not worth half a cent. All I can do is frown. Still, Chou has done the monk one better.
Right now I throw it down into West Lake;
    Only with the ability of Hsueh Tou could this be done. I don't want it either.
The pure wind of unburdening—to whom should it be imparted?
    From the past through the present. Tell me, is Hsueh Tou harmonizing with Chao Chou, or is he putting down footnotes for him? One son attains intimately.

COMMENTARY

Of Fen Yang's eighteen kinds of questions, this one in the Case is called a "wrapping-up question." Hsueh Tou says, "He wraps everything up and presses against the ancient old awl." He wraps up everything and makes it return to unity.

This monk wanted to press Chao Chou, but Chou too was an adept. Where it was impossible to turn, he had a way to show himself: daring to open his big mouth he immediately said, "When I was in Ch'ing Chou I made a cloth shirt that weighed seven pounds." Hsueh Tou says, "How many people can there be who know the weight of this seven-pound shirt?"

"Right now I throw it down into West Lake." Myriad things return to one, but he doesn't even need the one. Since he doesn't need the seven-pound cloth shirt either, all at once he

throws it down into West Lake. When Hsueh Tou dwelt on
Tung T'ing's green peak, there was a West Lake (nearby).

"The pure wind of unburdening—to whom should it be imparted?" This refers to Chao Chou teaching his assembly, saying, "If you're coming north I'll load up for you. If you're coming south I'll unload for you. Even if you're coming from Hsueh
Feng or Yun Chu, you're still a fellow carrying a board." Hsueh
Tou says, "To whom should a pure wind like this be imparted?" "Loading up" means speaking for you of mind and
nature, of mysteries and marvels—all sorts of expedient
methods. If it's unloaded, there are no longer so many meanings and hidden wonders.

Some people carried a load of Ch'an to Chao Chou's place,
but when they got there they couldn't make use of it at all. He
would set them straight all at once, making them free and easy,
without the slightest concern. We say of this, "After awakening it's the same as before awakening."

People these days all make unconcern an understanding.
Some say, "There is no delusion or enlightenment: it's not
necessary to go on seeking. Even before the Buddha appeared in
the world, before Bodhidharma ever came to this country, it
could not have been otherwise. What's the use of the Buddha
appearing in the world? What did the Patriarch still come from
the West for?" All such views—what relevance do they have?
You must have greatly penetrated and greatly awakened: then
as before, mountains are mountains, rivers are rivers, in fact all
the myriad things are perfectly manifest. Then for the first
time you can be an unconcerned person.

Haven't you heard Lung Ya say:

> To study the Path, first you must have a basis of
>   enlightenment:
> It's like having vied in a boat race:
> Though you relax on idle ground as before,
> Only having won can you rest.

As for this story of Chao Chou's seven-pound cloth shirt,
look how this man of old talks this way, like gold and jade. Me
talking like this, you listening like this—all of this is "loading
up." But say, what is unloading? Go back to your places and
look into this.

TRANSLATORS' NOTES

a. The story is told as follows in the *Ch'uan Teng Lun* 10:

When (his master) P'an Shan died, P'u Hua carried on his teaching in the north, sometimes in city markets, sometimes in isolated villages. He would ring his bell and say, "I hit whether you're coming from light or coming from darkness."

One day Lin Chi sent a monk to catch him by saying, "How is it when neither light nor dark?" P'u Hua answered, "Tomorrow there's a feast at the Temple of Great Compassion."

Ching Ch'ing's Sound of Raindrops

POINTER

With a single stroke he completes it and passes beyond ordinary and holy. His slightest word can break things up, untying what is bound and releasing what is stuck. As if walking on thin ice or running over sword blades, he sits within the heaps of sound and form, he walks on top of sound and form.

For the moment I leave aside wondrous functioning in all directions. How is it when he leaves that very instant? To test I'm citing this old case: look!

CASE

Ching Ch'ing asked a monk, "What sound is that outside the gate?"[1] The monk said, "The sound of raindrops."[2]

Ch'ing said, "Sentient beings are inverted. They lose themselves and follow after things."[3]

The monk said, "What about you, Teacher?"[4]

Ch'ing said, "I almost don't lose myself."[5]

The monk said, "What is the meaning of 'I almost don't lose myself'?"[6]

Ch'ing said, "Though it still should be easy to express oneself, to say the whole thing has to be difficult."[7]

NOTES

1. He casually lets down a hook. He doesn't suffer from deafness: what is he asking?
2. He's undeniably truthful. It's good news too.
3. A concern is born. Ch'ing is used to getting his way. He rakes the monk in. He depends on his own abilities.
4. As it turns out the monk suffers a defeat. He's turned the spear around: inevitably it will be hard for Ch'ing to stand up to it.

Instead (of Ch'ing, the monk) grabs the spear and stabs the man back.

5. Bah! He just can't explain.
6. He presses this old fellow and crushes the man. His first arrow was still light, the second arrow was deep.
7. Provisions to nourish a son. Although it's like this, where have Te Shan and Lin Chi gone? If he doesn't call it the sound of raindrops, what sound should he call it? It simply can't be explained.

COMMENTARY

You too should understand right here. When the Ancients imparted their teaching, with one device, one object, they wanted to guide people. One day Ching Ch'ing asked a monk, "What is that sound outside the gate?" The monk said, "The sound of quail." Ch'ing said, "If you wish to avoid uninterrupted hell, don't slander the Wheel of the True Dharma of the Tathagata." Another time Ch'ing asked, "What is that sound outside the gate?" A monk said, "The sound of a snake eating a frog." Ch'ing said, "I knew that sentient beings suffer: here is another suffering sentient being." These words are the same as the Case. If patchrobed monks can penetrate here, nothing can block their independence within the heaps of sound and form. If you can't penetrate then you are constrained by sound and form.

In various places they call this "tempering words." If it were tempering, it would only amount to mental activity. (Those with this view) do not see where the ancient man Ching Ch'ing helped people. (Ch'ing's words in the Case) are also called "penetrating sound and form," "explaining the eye of the Path," "explaining sound and form," "explaining the mind source," "explaining forgetting feelings," "explaining preaching." Though (such interpretations) are undeniably detailed, nevertheless they still are stuck in clichés.

When Ch'ing asked this way, "What is that sound outside the gate?" the monk said, "The sound of raindrops." But then Ch'ing said, "Sentient beings are inverted. They lose themselves and follow after things." People all misunderstand and call this intentionally upsetting the man, but this has nothing to do with it. How little they realize that Ch'ing has the skill to help people. Ch'ing is so brave he isn't bound by a single device and a single object. Above all he doesn't spare his eyebrows.

How could Ching Ch'ing not have known that it was the sound of raindrops? Why was it still worth asking? You must realize that the Ancient was using his probing pole and reed shade (to see into the depths) to examine this monk. The monk too pressed back well, immediately saying, "What about you, Teacher?" What happened then was that Ching Ch'ing went into the mud and water to say to him, "I almost don't lose myself." The reason (for saying this) was that the monk was losing himself, pursuing things. Why did Ching Ch'ing lose himself too? You must realize that Ch'ing had a place to get out himself within the phrase he used to test the monk.

This monk was very dull—he wanted to beat this statement into the ground, so he asked, "What is the meaning of 'I almost don't lose myself'?" If it had been the school of Te Shan or Lin Chi the blows and shouts would already have been falling. But Ching Ch'ing put through a single continuous path and followed him creating complications: he went on to say more to him, "Though it still should be easy to express oneself, to say the whole thing has to be difficult." Nevertheless, as an Ancient said, "Continuity is indeed very difficult." Ching Ch'ing illuminated for this monk the great affair under his feet.

Hsueh Tou's verse says:

VERSE

An empty hall, the sound of raindrops...
Never ever interrupted. Everyone is here.

Hard to respond, even for an adept.
Of course he doesn't know how. I have never been an
adept. There's provisional and real, there's letting go and
gathering in, there's killing and bringing to life, there's
catching and releasing.

If you say he's ever let the streams enter,
You stick your head into a bowl of glue. If you don't call it
the sound of raindrops, what sound will you call it?

As before you still don't understand.
How often I've asked you! You tubs of lacquer! Give me
back my holeless iron hammer.

Understanding or not understanding—
>Cut off the two ends. The two are not separate. It's not on these two sides.

On South Mountain, on North Mountain, more and more downpour.
>Above our heads and under our feet. If you call it the sound of raindrops, you're blind. If you don't call it the sound of raindrops, what sound will you call it? Your feet must be treading the ground of reality before you can get here.

COMMENTARY

"An empty hall, the sound of raindrops / Hard to respond, even for an adept." If you call it the sound of raindrops, then this is "losing oneself, following after things." If you don't call it the sound of raindrops, then how will you turn things around? At this point even if you're an adept, it's still hard to respond. Therefore an Ancient said, "If your view equals your teacher's, you have less than half the teacher's merit. Only if your view goes beyond your teacher's are you fit to receive and carry on the transmission." And as Nan Yuan said, "With acceptance of birthlessness under the cudgel, he faces situations without deferring to a teacher."

"If you say he ever let the streams enter, / As before you still don't understand." In the *Surangama Sutra* it says, "First, in the midst of hearing, (Avalokitesvara) let the streams enter, but was mindless of what was there. Since what he let in was quiescent, the two forms, motion and stillness, were ultimately not produced." If you say it's the sound of raindrops, it's not right, and if you say it's not the sound of raindrops, it's not right either. If you say he lets the streams of sound and form enter, that's not right either. If you call it sound and form, as before you don't understand his meaning. It is compared to pointing at the moon with one's finger: the moon is not the finger.

Understanding and not understanding, "On South Mountain, on North Mountain, more and more downpour."

Yun Men's Six Do Not Take It In

POINTER

What does the sky say? The four seasons go on there. What does the earth say? The myriad things are born there. Where the four seasons go on, he can see the essence; where the myriad things are born, he can see the action.

But say, where can you see a patchrobed monk? Having abandoned words and speech and active functioning, having blocked off your throat when walking, standing, sitting, and lying down—can you still discern him?

CASE

A monk asked Yun Men, "What is the Body of Reality?"[1a] Men said, "Six do not take it in."[2]

NOTES

1. So many people have doubts about this. The thousand sages can't leap out of it. He's indulged quite a bit.
2. He cuts nails and shears through iron. "An eight-corner mortar flies through the air." The spirit tortoise is dragging his tail.

COMMENTARY

Yun Men said, "Six do not take it in." This is indeed hard to understand: even if you reach it before the first indications are distinct, this is already the secondary. If you understand after the first indications arise, then you've fallen into the tertiary. If you go to the words and phrases to discern (his meaning), you will search without ever being able to find it.

But ultimately, what do you take as the Body of Reality? Those who are adepts immediately get up and go as soon as they hear it raised. If on the other hand you linger in thought and hold back your potential, you should listen humbly to this treatment.

The senior monk Fu of T'ai Yuan was originally a lecturer. One day when he had gone up to his seat to lecture, he spoke of the Body of Reality saying, "Vertically it reaches through the three times, and horizontally it extends through the ten directions." There was a Ch'an traveller in the audience who let out a laugh as he heard this. Fu came down from his seat and said, "What was my shortcoming just now? Please, Ch'an man, explain so I can see." The Ch'an man said, "Lecturer, you only lecture on that which pertains to the extent of the Body of Reality—you don't see the Body of Reality." Fu said, "After all, what would be right?" The Ch'an man said, "You should temporarily stop lecturing and sit in a quiet room. You have to see it for yourself."

Fu did as he said and sat quietly all night. Suddenly he heard them hitting the bell for the fifth watch: suddenly he was greatly enlightened. So he went and knocked on the Ch'an man's door saying, "I've understood." The Ch'an man said, "Try to say something so I can see." Fu said, "From today onwards I'll no longer twist these nostrils born of my parents."

Again: in the scriptures it says, "The Buddha's true Body of Reality is like empty space. It manifests shapes in response to things like the moon (reflected) in the water."

Again: a monk asked Chia Shan, "What is the Body of Reality?" Shan said, "The Body of Reality has no form." The monk asked, "What is the Eye of Reality?" Shan said, "The Eye of Reality has no flaws."

Yun Men said, "Six do not take it in." Some say of this case, "This is just the six sense-organs, the six sense-objects, the six consciousnesses. These sixes all arise from the Body of Reality, so the six faculties cannot take it in." Intellectual interpretations such as this, though, are irrelevant. Moreover, they drag down Yun Men. If you want to see, then see: there's no place for your attempts to rationalize. Haven't you seen how it says in the scripture: "This Truth is not something that calculating thought and discrimination can understand."

Yun Men's answers have often provoked people's intellectual interpretations. Thus in every phrase of Yun Men's there are inevitably three phrases present. Nor does he turn his back on your questions: responding to the time, adapting to the season, with one word, one phrase, one dot, one line, he indeed has a place to show himself. Thus it is said, "When a single phrase is penetrated, a thousand phrases, ten thousand phrases, are penetrated all at once."

But say, is "Six do not take it in" the Body of Reality? Is it the Patriarchs? I give you thirty blows!

Hsueh Tou's verse says:

VERSE

One, two, three, four, five, six—
    Go all the way through, then start again at the beginning. For every drop of water, a drop of ice. Why expend so much effort?

The blue-eyed barbarian monk can't count up to it.
    Past, present, and future lives for sixty eons. Have you ever seen Bodhidharma even in a dream? Why do you deliberately transgress?

Shao Lin deceptively said he passed it on to Shen Kuang—
    When one man transmits a falsehood, ten thousand transmit it as truth. From the start it was already wrong.

He rolled up his robe and said he was returning to India.
    He utterly swindled ordinary people. How embarrassing!

India is vast, there's no place to look for him—
    Where is he? This at last is the Great Peace. Right now, where is he?

He comes back by night to stay here at Ju Peak.
    He pokes out your eyes. Still, he's raising waves where there's no wind. But say, is it the Body of Reality or the Body of Buddha? I'll give you thirty blows!

COMMENTARY

Hsueh Tou is well able to show his eye where there is no seam or crack and come out with a verse to make people see. Yun Men said, "Six do not take it in." Why does Hsueh Tou nonetheless say, "One, two, three, four, five, six"? In fact not even the blue-eyed barbarian monk can count up to it. That is why it is said, "I just allow that the old barbarian knows—I don't allow that he understands." Only a descendant of Yun Men's house (like Hsueh Tou) could do this. I just said that Yun Men responds to the time and adapts to the season with one word, one phrase. Only if you can penetrate through will you know that the Path is not a matter of words and phrases. But if you're not yet this way, you won't avoid making up intellectual interpretations.

My late master Wu Tsu said, "Shakyamuni Buddha was a lowdown hired worker. The cypress trees in the garden: one, two, three, four, five." If you can manage truly to see under Yun Men's words, you'll reach this realm instantly.

"Shao Lin deceptively said he passed it on to Shen Kuang." The Second Patriarch's initial name was Shen Kuang. Later he said that Bodhidharma had returned to India. Bodhidharma had been buried at the foot of Bear Ears Mountain. At that time the (Liu) Sung emissary Yun Feng was returning from the West. In the Western Mountains he saw Bodhidharma carrying one shoe in his hand going back to India. The emissary returned and reported this to the Emperor. When Bodhidharma's tomb was opened they only saw a single shoe left behind.

Hsueh Tou says, "How can this matter really be imparted?" Since there was no imparting it, Bodhidharma rolled up his robe and said he was returning to India. But then tell me, why has this country nevertheless had six patriarchs handing it on in succession this way? Here it's unavoidably obscure. You must be able to comprehend before you can enter and act.

"India is vast, there's no place to look for him— / He comes back by night to stay here at Ju Peak." But tell me, where is he right now?

Master Yuan Wu then struck saying, "Blind men!"

TRANSLATORS' NOTES

a. The Body of Reality (Dharmakaya) is called the real true body of all Buddhas, the most essential and most inclusive aspect of Buddhahood. Different elaborations on the nature of Dharmakaya have been made in the various schools of Buddhist thought and practice. Sometimes it is said to comprise two complementary aspects, knowledge and principle, meaning realization of the inherent pattern that matter-energy is one with a void like empty space. The infinite universe or cosmos itself can be seen as the Dharmakaya of True Suchness, represented in the esoteric schools as the manifestation of Vairocana Buddha, the universal illuminator, the so-called Adibuddha or Primordial Buddha. According to esoteric Buddhist teaching, the exoteric schools regard the Dharmakaya as being unmanifest and inexpressible, whereas the esoteric schools see that it is also manifest and expressive. As in the present case, Ch'an Buddhism sees both sides of this. Seng Chao, the great sage of the Middle Path school, quoted several times in this case, said that the Dharmakaya is uncompounded and is not contained in sets of classification or enumeration. See also Cases 39 and 82.

Turning Over the Tea Kettle at Chao Ch'ing

CASE

When Minister Wang entered Chao Ch'ing, they were making tea.[1] At the time Elder Lang was holding the kettle for Ming Chao.[2] Lang turned the tea kettle over.[3] Seeing this, the Minister asked the Elder, "What's under the tea stove?"[4] Lang said, "The spirit who holds up stoves."[5] The Minister said, "If it's the spirit who holds up stoves, why then did you turn over the tea kettle?"[6] Lang said, "Serve as an official for a thousand days, lose it in a single morning."[7] The Minister shook out his sleeves and left.[8]

Ming Chao said, "Elder Lang, you've eaten Chao Ch'ing food, but still you go beyond the river to make noise gathering charred wood."[9] Lang said, "What about you, Teacher?"[10] Ming Chao said, "The spirit got the advantage."[11]

Hsueh Tou said, "At the time I just would have kicked over the tea stove."[12]

NOTES

1. A gathering of adepts: there's bound to be something extraordinary. Casual and unconcerned. Everyone set one eye on them. Wang has invited trouble.
2. A bunch of fellows playing with a mud ball. Lang doesn't know how to make tea, so he drags in someone else.
3. Something's happened after all.
4. As it turns out, it's trouble.
5. After all he runs into Wang's arrow. Nonetheless, it's extraordinary.
6. Why doesn't he give him some real provisions? Something's happened.

7. A mistaken indication. What kind of talk is this? Phoney Ch'an men are (as numerous) as hemp seeds, as millet grains.
8. Obviously an adept. I allow that he has one eye.
9. I would go on to give him thirty blows. This lone-eye dragon only has one eye. Still, it takes a clear-eyed man to examine thoroughly.
10. He presses him—he too deserves to be pressed. Never make up such dead senile views!
11. After all, he only has one eye. He was able to speak half. One hand presses down, one hand lifts up.
12. What can be done about it? He draws his bow after the thief has gone. Nonetheless, he still can't be called a member of Te Shan's school. The lot of them, (Wang, Lang, and Ming Chao) are rascals, scoundrels—among them Hsueh Tou is the stand-out.

COMMENTARY

Minister Wang was in charge of Ch'uan Chou. He had studied at Chao Ch'ing for a long time. One day he went into the temple while Elder Lang was making tea, and Lang turned over the tea kettle. The Minister too was an adept. As soon as he saw him turn over the tea kettle he immediately asked the Elder, "What is under the tea stove?" When Lang said, "The spirit who holds up stoves," inevitably there was an echo in his words. But what could he do about his head and tail contradicting each other, so that he lost the source meaning and blundered with the sharp point, cutting his own hand? Not only did he wrong himself, but he also offended the other man.

Though this is an affair without gain and loss, if we bring it up, as before there is near and far, initiate and outsider. If you discuss this matter, though it's not in words and phrases, nevertheless you must discern what's alive in the words and phrases. Thus it is said, "He only studies the living phrase; he doesn't study the dead phrase."

When Elder Lang talked this way he was like a mad dog chasing a clod of dirt. The Minister shook out his sleeves and left, appearing to disapprove of him.

Ming Chao said, "Elder Lang, you've eaten Chao Ch'ing food, but still you go beyond the river to make noise gathering charred wood." This charred wood is sticks of wood burnt by fire in the wild. Ming Chao used this to illustrate how Elder Lang didn't go to the correct place to walk, but instead ran off outside. Lang pressed him saying, "What about you, Teacher?" Ming Chao said, "The spirit got the advantage." Naturally Ming Chao had a place to show himself without turning his back on Lang's question. Thus it is said, "A good dog bites in without showing his teeth."

Master Che of Kuei Shan said, "Minister Wang was like Hsiang Ju[a] carrying off the jewel—in fact his sideburns were sticking out from under his hat." Since Ming Chao couldn't contain his feelings, it was difficult for him to do what was proper. If I had been Elder Lang, as soon as I saw the Minister shake out his sleeves and go, I would have let go of the tea kettle and laughed out loud. Why? If you see him but don't grab him, it's hard to meet with him even in a thousand years."

If you wish to know the meaning of the Buddha-nature, you must observe times and seasons, causes and conditions. Haven't you heard? Pao Shou asked Nail Cutter Hu, "For a long time I've heard of Nail Cutter Hu—aren't you him?" Hu said, "I am." Shou said, "Can you drive nails into empty space?" Hu said, "I invite the Master to come smash it." Shou then hit him. Hu did not agree, so Shou said, "Another day there will be a talkative teacher who will examine this thoroughly for you." Later Hu saw Chao Chou and related the previous conversation. Chou said, "Why were you hit by him?" Hu said, "I don't know where the fault was." Chou said, "You couldn't even do anything about this one crack, yet you went on to tell him to break up empty space." At this Hu was stopped—Chou spoke for him, "Well, nail up this one crack." At this Hu had an awakening.

When Seven Masters Mi of Ching Chao returned from his foot travels, an old adept asked him, "A piece of well-rope on a moonlit night—people all called it a snake. I wonder what you call it, Seven Masters, when you see the Buddha." Seven Masters said, "If there is something seen, then it's the same as sentient beings." The old adept said, "This is a peach pit that sprouts once in a thousand years."

National Teacher Chung asked the purple-clad Imperial Attendant Monk, "I hear tell that you have (written a commentary) explaining the 'Consideration of Benefit' Scripture. Is this so or not?" The Imperial Attendant said, "It is so." The National Teacher said, "One must first understand the Buddha's meaning to be fit to explain the scriptures." The Imperial Attendant said, "If I didn't understand the meaning, how could I dare to say I've explained the Scripture?" The National Teacher then ordered the servant to bring a bowl of water, seven grains of rice, and a single chopstick. Putting them in the bowl, he passed it to the Imperial Attendant and asked, "What meaning is this?" The Imperial Attendant said, "I don't understand." The National Teacher said, "You don't even understand my meaning: how can you go on talking of Buddha's meaning?"

(So we see) Minister Wang and Elder Lang were not the only ones to have conversations like this.

At the end Hsueh Tou turns around and says, "At the time I just would have kicked over the tea stove." Though Ming Chao was like this, he never equalled Hsueh Tou. Hsueh Feng was the cook in Tung Shan's congregation. One day when he was sifting rice, Tung Shan asked, "What are you doing?" Feng said, "Sifting rice." Shan said, "Do you sift the rice to get rid of the grit, or do you sift the grit and get rid of the rice?" Feng said, "Grit and rice are both removed at once." Shan said, "What will the great congregation eat?" Feng turned the bowl over. Shan said, "The right conditions for you are not here." Though he acted this way, how can this compare with Hsueh Tou saying, "At the time I just would have kicked over the tea stove"? What time and season was it for them? Their action naturally stands out in the present and shines through the ages: they had a place of living liberation.

The verse says:

VERSE

(Wang) poses a question like creating a wind—
  His arrow was not shot in vain. He happens to be artful yet quintessential.
(Lang's) responsive action was not skillful.
  Fellows playing with a mud ball—what end is there to it? A square peg stuck in a round hole. Indeed, he ran into an adept.

How lamentable! the lone-eyed dragon (Ming Chao)
He only has one eye. He only gets one part.

Didn't display his teeth and claws.
Indeed he had no teeth and claws that could have been
displayed. What teeth and claws are you talking about?
Don't cheat them.

Teeth and claws open
Do you see? After all Hsueh Tou has gotten somewhere. If
you have such ability, kick over the tea stove!

Producing clouds and thunder.
All the world's people take a beating at once. The world's
patchrobed monks have no place to put themselves.
Crashing thunder in a parched sky.

How many times I've gone through the waves of adverse cur-
rents!
Seventy-two blows turns into a hundred and fifty.

COMMENTARY

"Posing a question like creating a wind— / The responsive action was not skillful." The Minister's question was not skillful." The Minister's question was like swinging an axe (so
swiftly that) it creates a wind. This comes from (a story in)
Chuang Tzu: a man of Ying was plastering a wall. Only one
small gap remained, so he threw a gob of plaster on to fill it in,
whereupon a bit of plaster splashed down onto the tip of his
nose. Nearby was an axeman who said, "You filled that hole
very skillfully. I'll wield my axe and take that plaster off the tip
of your nose for you." Though the plaster on his nose was (as
small as) a fly speck, he let him remove it. The axeman swung
his axe so fast he created a wind and removed the plaster entirely without cutting his nose. The man of Ying stood there
without losing his composure. This is what is called wondrous
skill on the part of both. Though Elder Lang did respond to
Minister Wang's actions, his words were without excellent
skillfulness. That's why Hsueh Tou said, "(Wang) poses a question like creating a wind / (Lang's) responsive action was not
skillful."

"How lamentable: the lone-eyed dragon / Didn't display his teeth and claws." Ming Chao speaking was indeed very outstanding. Nevertheless, he didn't have the teeth and claws to grasp clouds and hold onto fog. The bystander Hsueh Tou didn't approve. Not containing his feeling, he showed some energy on behalf of Ming Chao.

Hsueh Tou secretly goes to merge with Minister Wang's meaning. He versifies his own statement about kicking over the tea stove: "Teeth and claws open / Producing clouds and thunder / How many times I've gone through the waves of adverse currents!" Yun Men said, "I don't expect you to have waves that go against the current. Just have the mind that goes along with the current and you'll be all right too." Thus it is said, "If you comprehend at the living phrase, you'll never forget." The words and phrases of Elder Lang and of Ming Chao seem dead. If you want to see the living place, just look at Hsueh Tou kicking over the tea stove.

TRANSLATORS' NOTES

a. "Hsiang Ju carrying off the jewel"—During the Warring States Period, Lian Hsiang Ju was a minister of the state of Chao, sent to Ch'in to exchange a precious jewel for fifteen cities. Suspecting that the King of Ch'in didn't intend to keep the bargain to turn over the fifteen cities, Hsiang Ju managed to get out of Ch'in and return the jewel safely to his master the King of Chao.

San Sheng's Golden Fish Who Has Passed through the Net

POINTER

Piercing, penetrating, one takes the drum and captures the flag. Fortified, entrenched, one inspects the front and oversees the rear.

One who sits on the tiger's head to take the tiger's tail is not yet an adept. Though an ox head disappears and a horse head returns, this too is not yet extraordinary.

But say, how is it when a man who has passed beyond measurements comes? To test I'm citing this old case: look!

CASE

San Sheng asked Hsueh Feng, "I wonder, what does the golden fish who has passed through the net use for food?"[1]

Feng said, "When you come out of the net I'll tell you."[2]

Sheng said, "The teacher of fifteen-hundred people and you don't even know what to say!"[3]

Feng said, "My affairs as abbot are many and complicated."[4]

NOTES

1. (The golden fish) is free in all ways. This question is too lofty. You must just know for yourself—then what need is there to ask any further?
2. He diminishes the other man's reputation quite a bit. An expert teacher of our sect is naturally independent.
3. The crashing noise of sudden thunder really startles the crowd. Let him leap about.
4. It's not a matter of victory and defeat. Hsueh Feng lets his move go. This statement is most poisonous.

COMMENTARY

With Hsueh Feng and San Sheng, though there's one exit and one entry, one thrust and one parry, there is no division into victory and defeat. But say, what is the eye that these two venerable adepts possess?

San Sheng received the secret from Lin Chi. He travelled all over and everyone treated him as an eminent guest. Look at him posing a question. How many people look but cannot find him! He doesn't touch on inherent nature or the Buddha Dharma: instead he asks, "What does the golden fish who has passed through the net use for food?" But say, what was his meaning? Since the golden fish who has passed through the net ordinarily does not eat the tasty food of others, what does he use for food?

Hsueh Feng is an adept: in a casual fashion he replies to San Sheng with only ten or twenty percent. He just said to him, "When you come out of the net, I'll tell you." Fen Yang would call this "a question that displays one's understanding." In the Ts'ao Tung tradition it would be called "a question that uses things." You must be beyond categories and classifications, you must have obtained the use of the great function, you must have an eye on your forehead—only then can you be called a golden fish who has passed through the net. Nevertheless, Hsueh Feng is an adept and can't help but diminish the other man's reputation by saying "When you come out of the net, I'll tell you."

Observe how the two of them held fast to their territories, towering up like ten thousand fathom walls. With this one sentence of Hsueh Feng's anyone other than San Sheng would have been unable to go on. Yet San Sheng too was an adept: thus he knew how to say to him, "The teacher of fifteen hundred people and you don't even know what to say!" But Hsueh Feng said, "My affairs as abbot are many and complicated." How obstinate this statement is!

When these adepts met, there was one capture and one release—(each) acted weak when encountering strength and acted noble when encountering meanness. If you form your understanding in terms of victory and defeat, you haven't seen Hsueh Feng even in dreams. Look at these two men: initially both were solitary and dangerous, lofty and steep; in the end both were dead and decrepit. But say, was there still gain and loss, victory and defeat? When these adepts harmonized with each other, it was necessarily not this way.

San Sheng was the Temple Keeper at Lin Chi. When Lin Chi was about to pass on he directed, "After I'm gone you mustn't destroy the treasure of the eye of my correct teaching." San Sheng came forward and said, "How could we dare destroy the treasure of the eye of your correct teaching, Master?" Chi said, "In the future, how will you act when people ask questions?" San Sheng then shouted. Chi said, "Who would have known that the treasure of the eye of my correct teaching would perish in this blind donkey?" San Sheng then bowed in homage. Since he was a true son of Lin Chi's, he dared to respond like this.

Afterwards Hsueh Tou just versifies the golden fish who has passed through the net, revealing where these adepts saw each other. The verse says:

VERSE

The golden fish who has passed through the net—
> A thousand soldiers are easy to get, but one general is hard to find. What is the golden fish like? The thousand sages can't do anything about it.

Stop saying he tarries in the water.
> He stands beyond the clouds, leaping with life. But better not make him out to be a fool.

He shakes the heavens and sweeps the earth,
> An adept! An adept! This still isn't where he's extraordinary. Let him come out (of the net)—what's to prevent it?

He flourishes his mane and wags his tail.
> Who would presume to judge the whole from the surface? He's performed a clever trick and startled the crowd.

When a thousand-foot whale spouts, vast waves fly,
> San Sheng revolved over to That Side: he is indeed outstanding! He's swallowed everyone in the world in a single gulp.

At a single thunderclap, the pure wind gusts.
> Having eyes and ears, but being like blind and deaf. Who is not frightened?

The pure wind gusts—
   Where? Bah!

Among gods and humans, how many know? How many?
   Hsueh Feng holds down the front lines, San Sheng holds
down the rear. Why scatter dust and sand? I'll hit and say,
"Where are you?"

COMMENTARY

"The golden fish who has passed through the net— / Stop saying he tarries in the water." Wu Tsu said that just this one
couplet alone completes the verse. Since it's the golden fish
who has passed through the net, how could he linger tarrying
in the water? He must be where the vast swelling floods of
white foamy waves tower up to the skies. But say, during the
twenty-four hours of the day, what does he use for food? All of
you go back to your places and try to see for sure.

Hsueh Tou said, "This matter is picked up and played with
according to one's capacity." When something like the golden
fish "flourishes his mane and wags his tail," he does in fact
shake heaven and earth.

"When a thousand-foot whale spouts, vast waves fly." This
versifies San Sheng saying, "The teacher of fifteen hundred
people and you don't even know what to say!" He was like a
whale spouting out giant waves. "At a single thunderclap, the
pure wind gusts." This versifies Hsueh Feng saying, "My affairs as abbot are many and complicated." He was like the pure
wind gusting when a thunderclap sounds. The overall meaning
is to praise the two of them for both being adepts.

"The pure wind gusts— / Among gods and humans, how
many know? How many?" But say, what do these lines come
down to? When the pure wind arises, among gods and humans
how many can there be who will know?

Yun Men's Every Atom Samadhi

POINTER

Passing beyond stages, absolutely transcending expedient means, mind to mind in mutual accord, each phrase harmonizing with the other. If you haven't entered the gate of great liberation and attained great liberty of action, how can you measure the Buddhas and Patriarchs, or be a mirror and guide for the Essential Vehicle?

But say, when taking charge of a situation directly, whether going with or going against, whether vertically or horizontally, how will you be able to speak a phrase to express yourself? To test, I'm citing this old case: look!

CASE

A monk asked Yun Men, "What is every atom samadhi?"[1] Men said, "Food in the bowl, water in the bucket."[2]

NOTES

1. All the monks under heaven make their nests here. His whole mouth is filled with frost. Why is he scattering sand and dirt?
2. A cloth bag filled with awls. Gold dust and sand intermingled. He adds error to error. Inside the palace, they don't ask about the capital.

COMMENTARY

Can you settle this case properly? If you can, then Yun Men's nostrils are in your hands. If you are unable to settle it properly, then your nostrils are in Yun Men's hands. Yun Men has phrases that cut nails and shear through iron. In this one phrase three phrases are present.

When questioned about this case, some say, "Each grain of the food in the bowl is round; each drop of the water in the bucket is wet." If you understand in this fashion, then you don't see how Yun Men really helped the man.

The verse says:

VERSE

"Food in the bowl, water in the bucket"—
> It's obvious. Why scatter sand and dirt? You must wash your mouth out for three years before you'll get it.

The talkative teacher can hardly open his mouth.
> He draws in his tongue. Those who know the law fear it. Why then bring it up this way?

Northern Dipper, Southern Star—their positions are not different:
> Why call east west? Sitting, standing, still and solemn. What's long is the long Body of Reality; what's short is the short Body of Reality.

White foamy waves flooding the skies arise on level ground.
> Several fathoms deep underfoot. Guest and host interchange. Suddenly they're on top of your head—what will you do? I hit.

Trying or not trying,
> Heavens! Bah!

Stopping or not stopping,
> What are you saying, Hsueh Tou? You are adding more hatred and bitterness.

Each and every one is a rich man's son with no britches.
> Quite decrepit! The onlooker laughs at them.

COMMENTARY

Previously, in his verse on (Case 14) 'Yun Men's An Appropriate Statement,' Hsueh Tou said, "An appropriate statement / How utterly unique! / He wedges a stake into the iron hammer head with no handle hole." Later, in his verse on (Case 73) 'Ma

Tsu's Beyond All the Permutations of Assertion and Denial,' he says, "Tsang's head is white, Hai's head is black / Clear-eyed patchrobed monks cannot understand." If you are able to penetrate these cases, then you will see this present verse.

At the start Hsueh Tou immediately says, "Food in the bowl, water in the bucket." There's an echo in his words; he shows his capacity in the line. "The talkative teacher can hardly open his mouth." With this he adds footnotes for you. If you demand rational calculations here of the mysterious and the wondrous, it will be even harder to open your mouths.

At the beginning he holds fast. Fearing that there would be someone with eyes in the assembly who would see through him, later he had to forego the primary and bend down to open it up for beginners, coming out with a verse to make people see. As before the Northern Dipper is in the north and the Southern Star is in the south. Thus he says, "Northern Dipper, Southern Star—their positions are not different."

"White foamy waves flooding the skies arise on level ground." When waves suddenly arise on level ground, what will you do? If you catch sight of it in the phenomena, then it's easy. If you seek for it in your conceptual faculty, then you will never be able to find it. This line is like an iron spike: it can't be pulled out, and you can't get your beak into it. If you try to discuss it, though you wish to understand, you won't understand; though you wish to stop, you won't stop wildly displaying your load of ignorance. This is precisely (what is meant by) "Each and every one is a rich man's son with no britches."

Han Shan's poem says:

> Everywhere constantly suffering pain,
> All over vainly discussing themselves,
> Though they have talent, it's abandoned in the
>   weedy swamps;
> Having no power, they shut their reed doors.
> The sun comes up over the cliff, but still it's dark,
> The mist melts away, but the valley is still dim.
> The rich men's sons there
> Are all without britches.

Hsueh Feng's What Is It?

POINTER

As soon as there is affirmation and denial, you lose your mind in confusion. If you don't fall into grades and stages, then there is no seeking.

But say, is letting go right, or is holding fast right? At this point, if you have any trace of an interpretative route, you are still stuck in verbal explanations. If you're still involved with devices and objects, then all of this is haunting the fields and forests.[a]

Even if you arrive immediately at the point of solitary liberation, you haven't avoided looking back to the village gate from ten thousand miles away. Can you reach it? If you can't, just comprehend this perfectly obvious public case. To test I am citing it: look!

CASE

When Hsueh Feng was living in a hut, there were two monks who came to pay their respects.[1] Seeing them coming, he pushed open the door of the hut with his hand, popped out, and said, "What is it?"[2] A monk also said, "What is it?"[3] Feng lowered his head and went back inside the hut.[4]

Later the monk came to Yen T'ou.[5] T'ou asked, "Where are you coming from?"[6] The monk said, "I've come from Ling Nan."[7] T'ou said, "Did you ever go to Hsueh Feng?"[8] The monk said, "I went there."[9] T'ou said, "What did he have to say?" The monk recounted the preceding story.[10] T'ou said, "What did he say?"[11] The monk said, "He said nothing; he lowered his head and went back inside the hut."[12] T'ou said, "Alas! It's too bad I didn't tell him the last word before;[13] if I had told him, no one on earth could cope with old Hsueh."[14]

At the end of the summer the monk again brought up the preceding story to ask for instruction.[15] T'ou said, "Why didn't you ask earlier?"[16] The monk said, "I didn't dare to be casual."[17] T'ou said, "Though Hsueh Feng is born of the same lineage as me, he doesn't die in the same lineage as me.[18] If you want to know the last word, just this is it."[19]

NOTES

1. What for? Their crimes are listed on the same indictment.
2. Ghost eyes. A flute with no holes. He raises his head, wearing horns.
3. A mud ball. A felt-pounding board. The arrow points meet.
4. There are thorns in the soft mud. Hsueh Feng is like a dragon without feet, like a snake with horns. This is the hardest of all to handle.
5. He had to ask before he could understand. Only one on the same path would know.
6. It takes an adept to be able to be this way. This (monk) suffers defeat again and again. If Yen T'ou wasn't a fellow student of Hsueh Feng he probably would have let him go.
7. What news does he bring? He must convey the news. Did he see Hsueh Feng?
8. He already exposed him a while ago. He mustn't say he didn't go there.
9. A truthful man is hard to find. He breaks it in two.
10. So he goes on this way. Again and again he suffers defeat.
11. He should have hit the monk in the mouth, (but instead) he's lost his nostrils.
12. Again he suffers defeat. But tell me, what is he?
13. Vast swelling billows of white foamy waves flooding the skies.
14. A leper drags along his companions. Not necessarily. Even Mt. Sumeru would be shattered to bits. But say, where is his trap?
15. Already this monk is not alert. When the real thief has already been gone for quite a while, he draws his bow.
16. He deserves to have his meditation seat overturned. He's gone by.
17. This staff was originally for the monk to be beaten with. Yen T'ou pierced his nostrils. An imprisoned man increases in wisdom. It's already a double case.
18. He fills the heavens and covers the earth.
19. Though he utterly swindles ordinary people, I don't believe him. He almost couldn't complain.

COMMENTARY

Whoever would uphold the teaching of our school must discern how to take charge of the situation; he must know advance and retreat, right and wrong; he must understand killing and giving life, capturing and releasing. If one's eyes suddenly blur and go sightless, everywhere he goes, when he encounters a question, he questions, and when he encounters an answer, he answers, scarcely realizing that his nostrils are in the hands of others.

As for Hsueh Feng and Yen T'ou, they were fellow students under Te Shan. When these monks called on Hsueh Feng their views only reached to such a place (as seen in the case); when the monk saw Yen T'ou, he still didn't complete his business. He troubled these two worthies to no purpose. One question, one answer, one capture, one release—right up till today this case has been impenetrably obscure and inexplicable for everyone in the world. But tell me, where is it impenetrable and obscure?

Though Hsueh Feng had travelled all over through the various localities, at last it was at Tortoise Mountain because Yen T'ou spurred him on that he finally attained annihilation of doubt and great penetration.

Later, due to a purge, Yen T'ou became a ferryman by the shores of Lake O Chu (in Hupeh). On each shore hung a board: when someone wanted to cross, he would knock on the board. T'ou would call out, "Which side are you crossing to?" Then he would wave his oar and come out from among the reeds.

(After his enlightenment with Yen T'ou) Hsueh Feng returned to Ling Nan and lived in a hut. These monks were people who had studied for a long time. When he saw them coming, Hsueh Feng pushed open the door of the hut, popped out and said, "What is it?" Some people these days when questioned in this way immediately go and gnaw on his words. But these monks were unusual too; they just said to him "What is it?" Feng lowered his head and went back into the hut. This is frequently called "wordless understanding;" hence, these monks couldn't find him. Some say that, having been questioned by these monks, Hsueh Feng was in fact speechless, and so he returned to the hut. How far they are from knowing that there is something deadly poisonous in Hsueh Feng's intention. Though Hsueh Feng gained the advantage, nevertheless while he hid his body, he revealed his shadow.

Later one monk left Hsueh Feng and took this case to have Yen T'ou decide it. Once he got there, Yen T'ou asked him, "Where are you coming from?" The monk said, "I've come from Ling Nan." T'ou said, "Did you get to Hsueh Feng?" If you want to see Hsueh Feng, you better hurry up and look at this question. The monk said, "I went there." T'ou said, "What did he have to say?" This question was not posed to no purpose. But the monk did not understand: he just turned around following the trend of his words. T'ou said, "What did he say?" The monk said, "He lowered his head and went back into the hut without saying anything." This monk was far from knowing that Yen T'ou had put on straw sandals and had already walked around inside his belly several times.

Yen T'ou said, "Too bad I didn't tell him the last word before; if I had told him, no one on earth could cope with old Hsueh." Yen T'ou too supports the strong but doesn't help the weak. As before the monk was flooded with darkness and didn't distinguish initiate from naive. Harboring a bellyful of doubt, he really thought that Hsueh Feng did not understand.

At the end of the summer he again brought up this story and asked Yen T'ou for more instruction. T'ou said, "Why didn't you ask earlier?" This old fellow was crafty. The monk said, "I didn't dare to be casual." T'ou said, "Though Hsueh Feng is born of the same lineage as me, he doesn't die in the same lineage as me. If you want to know the last word, just this is it." Yen T'ou indeed did not spare his eyebrows! In the end, how will all of you people understand?

Hsueh Feng was the cook in Te Shan's community. One day the noon meal was late; Te Shan took his bowl and went down to the teaching hall. Feng said, "The bell hasn't rung yet, the drum hasn't been sounded—where is this old fellow going with his bowl?" Without saying anything, Te Shan lowered his head and returned to his abbot's quarters. When Hsueh Feng took this up with Yen T'ou, T'ou said, "Even the great Te Shan doesn't understand the last word."

Te Shan heard of this and ordered his attendant to summon Yen T'ou to the abbot's quarters. Shan said, "So you don't approve of me?" T'ou tacitly indicated what he meant. The next day Shan went up to the hall and taught in a way which was different from usual; in front of the monks' hall T'ou clapped his hands and laughed loudly saying, "Happily the old fellow does understand the last word! After this no one on earth will be able to do anything about him. Nevertheless, he's only got three years."

When Hsueh Feng saw Te Shan speechless, he thought that he had gained the advantage. He certainly didn't know that he had run into a thief. Since he had met a thief, later Feng too knew how to be a thief. Thus an Ancient said, "At the final word, one first reaches the impenetrable barrier."

Some say that Yen T'ou excelled Hsueh Feng; they have misunderstood. Yen T'ou always used this ability; he taught his community saying, "Clear-eyed folks have no clichés to nest in. Spurning things is considered superior, pursuing things is considered inferior. As for this last word, even if you've personally seen the Patriarchs, you still wouldn't be able to understand it rationally."

When Te Shan's noon meal was late, the old fellow picked up his bowl himself and went down to the teaching hall. Yen T'ou said, "Even great Te Shan doesn't understand the last word." Hsueh Tou picked this out and said, "I've heard that from the beginning a lone-eyed dragon has only one eye. You certainly didn't know that Te Shan was a toothless tiger. If it hadn't been for Yen T'ou seeing through him, how could we know that yesterday and today are not the same? Do all of you want to understand the last word? An Ancient said, 'I only allow that the old barbarian knows; I don't allow that he understands.'"

From ancient times up till now, the public cases have been extremely diverse, like a forest of brambles. If you can penetrate through, no one on earth can do anything about you, and all the Buddhas of past, present, and future defer to you. If you are unable to penetrate, study Yen T'ou saying, "Though Hsueh Feng is born in the same lineage as me, he doesn't die in the same lineage as me." Spontaneously, in just this one sentence, he had a way to express himself.

VERSE

The last word
    It's already present before any words. You think it's real.
    If you look right now at it, you'll go blind.

Is spoken for you;
> The tongue falls to the ground. It can't be spoken. It has a head but no tail; it has a tail but no head.

The time of light and dark pair by pair:
> Hsueh Tou is an old fellow who's full of complications. Like an ox without horns, like a tiger with horns. This one and that one are this way.

Born of the same lineage, they share the knowledge,
> What clan is this? There's no connection between this one and that one. You're headed southeast, I'm headed northwest.

Dying of different lineages, they're utterly separated.
> The staff is in my hand. How can you blame me? Why are your nostrils in someone else's hands?

Utterly separated—
> Do you want to take a beating? Where is there to search?

Even Yellow Head (Buddha) and Blue Eyes (Bodhidharma) have yet to discern.
> Everyone on earth loses his point and is tongue-tied. I too am this way; nevertheless, others are not. "I only allow that the old barbarian knows; I don't allow that he understands."

South, North, East, West, let us return—
> Hsueh Tou has gathered everyone in. His trail is still following the Five-Color Thread (leading to paradise). I ask you for a staff.

And in the depths of the night together look at the snow on the thousand crags.
> They still have half a month's journey. Let the world be covered with snow, filling the channels and gullies. There is no one who understands. You too are just blind people: do you know the last word? I'll hit!

COMMENTARY

"The last word is spoken for you." When Hsueh Tou made up his verse on this last word, he intentionally went to extremes falling into the weeds to help people. His verse was thoroughgoing as a verse, but he only versified a little of the fine detail. If you want to see all the way through, this is still not enough.

Daring to say even more, Hsueh Tou opened his big mouth and said, "The time of light and dark pair by pair" to open a road for you and also to finish it off for you in one line. Then at the end he provided even more explanations for you. Just as Chao Ch'ing one day asked Lo Shan, "When Yen T'ou says, 'So, so, not so, not so,' what is his meaning?" Lo Shan called out, "Great Master," and Master Chao Ch'ing responded. Shan said, "Both light and both dark." Ch'ing bowed in thanks and left. Three days later he again questioned Lo Shan, "A few days ago I received your compassionate instruction; it's just that I couldn't see through it." Shan said, "I've told you the whole thing already." Ch'ing said, "Master, please light the way." Shan said, "If so, Great Master, go ahead and ask about what you are in doubt over." Ch'ing said, "What is 'both light and both dark'?" Shan said, "Born the same and dying the same." Then Ch'ing bowed in thanks and left.

Later there was a monk who asked Chao Ch'ing, "How is it when being born the same and dying the same?" Ch'ing said, "Shut your dog mouth." The monk said, "Try to eat food with your mouth closed, Great Master." This monk then came to ask Lo Shan, "How is it when being born the same and dying the same?" Shan said, "Like an ox without horns." The monk asked, "How is it when being born the same but not dying the same?" Shan said, "Like a tiger with horns." The last word is precisely this truth.

There was a monk in Lo Shan's congregation who used this idea to put a question to Chao Ch'ing. Ch'ing said, "This one, this one, they all know. Why? If I spoke a phrase on the eastern continent, they would know it on the western continent too. If I spoke a phrase in heaven, in the human world they would also know it. All minds know each other, all eyes shine on each other."

Born of the same lineage, they're still easy to see. Not dying in the same lineage, they're utterly separate, and not even Shakyamuni or Bodhidharma can find them.

"South, North, East, West, let us return." There's something of a good world. "And in the depths of night together look at the snow on the thousand crags." But say, is this "both light and both dark" or is it "born of the same lineage" or is it "dying

in the same lineage"? Patchrobed monks who have eyes should
try to discern.

TRANSLATORS' NOTES

a. The image here is of ghosts clinging to trees and grasses, likened
    to people clinging to things, especially to words and expressions.

Chao Chou Lets Asses Cross, Lets Horses Cross

CASE

A monk asked Chao Chou, "For a long time I've heard of the stone bridge of Chao Chou, but now that I've come here I just see a simple log bridge."[1]

Chou said, "You just see the log bridge; you don't see the stone bridge."[2]

The monk said, "What is the stone bridge?"[3]

Chou said, "It lets asses cross, it lets horses cross."[4]

NOTES

1. Here's another man who comes to grab the tiger's whiskers. This is the proper business of patchrobed monks.
2. Chou is accustomed to getting the advantage. This old fellow is selling off his body.
3. He's climbed up onto Chou's hook, after all.
4. A single net cast over "asses" and "horses." In fact all the people in the world have no place to breathe; once dead they don't come back to life again.

COMMENTARY

In (the place) Chao Chou there's a stone bridge; ever since it was built (in the Latter Han dynasty) by Li Ying, it has been famous throughout the country. A simple log bridge is a bridge (made of) a single log.

Intentionally downgrading (Chao Chou's) grandeur, this monk questioned him saying, "For a long time I've heard of the stone bridge of Chao Chou, but now that I've come here I just see a simple log bridge." Chou immediately said, "You just see the log bridge, but you don't see the stone bridge," based on the other man's question. This seems just like ordinary conversation, but Chao Chou used it to hook him. This monk after all climbed onto the hook; he followed up behind and asked, "What is the stone bridge?" Chou said, "It lets asses cross, it lets horses cross." Inevitably Chao Chou naturally has a place to show himself in his words. Chao Chou is not like Lin Chi or Te Shan, carrying on with blows and shouts—he just uses words and speech to kill and bring to life.

Take a good look at this case. It seems to be an ordinary battle of wits; it is nevertheless hard to approach.

One day Chao Chou was with the head monk looking at the stone bridge when he asked the head monk, "Who built this?" The head monk said, "Li Ying built it." Chou said, "When he built it, where did he start?" The head monk had no reply. Chou said, "You're always talking about the stone bridge, but when you're asked about where it was started, you don't even know."

Also one day when Chao Chou was sweeping the floor, a monk asked, "Teacher, you are a man of knowledge—why is there dust?" Chou said, "It's something that comes from outside." Again the monk asked, "In a pure and clean monastery, why is there dust?" Chou said, "There's another little bit."

Also a monk asked, "What is the Path?" Chou said, "It's outside the wall." The monk said, "I'm not asking about that path, I'm asking about the Great Way." Chou said, "The Great Way runs through the capital."

Chao Chou was partial to using such devices; he would go to the safe secure place of ordinary reality to help people. He never cut his hand on the sharp point; naturally he was solitary and lofty, using these devices most wondrously.

Hsueh Tou's verse says,

VERSE

He doesn't set up the solitary and dangerous; in that his path
    is lofty.
    You must get to this realm before you realize. The words
    are still in our ears. This goes back to his own provisions.

Entering the ocean, he must hook a giant tortoise.
> He cuts off the essential crossing place and doesn't let
> profane or holy pass. Shrimps or clams, snails or oysters
> aren't worth asking about. People of power don't come by
> twos and threes.

His contemporary the Elder of Kuan Hsi is worth a laugh;
> There's been another such man who's come this way,
> who had such ability to use active devices.

Though he knew how to say "Whistling Arrow," his effort was
> *in vain.*
> He still has half a month's journey. He seems to resemble,
> but isn't really.

COMMENTARY

"He doesn't set up the solitary and dangerous; in that his path
is lofty." Hsueh Tou is praising Chao Chou's usual way of
helping people. Chou doesn't establish mysteries or marvels,
and doesn't set up the solitary and dangerous. He isn't like
those in various places who say that only breaking up empty
space, smashing Mount Sumeru to bits, producing dust on the
bottom of the ocean and pounding waves on Mount Sumeru
can be called the Path of the Patriarchal Teachers. Thus Hsueh
Tou says, "He doesn't set up the solitary and dangerous; in that
his path is lofty." Others may tower up like ten-mile-high
walls to display the extraordinary spiritual effects of the
Buddha Dharma—but though they're solitary and dangerous,
lofty and steep, this is not as good as not setting up the solitary
and dangerous, and simply acting ordinary, naturally turning
smoothly. Chao Chou doesn't establish anything, yet he is established himself; he doesn't make anything high, yet he is
high himself. When capacity goes beyond solitary and dangerous, only then do we see profound wonders.

Thus Hsueh Tou says, "Entering the ocean, he must hook a
giant tortoise." Look at Chao Chou: a master of our school
with eyes, he is perfectly at ease as he imparts a word and
employs a device. He doesn't hook shrimps or clams, snails or
oysters—he only hooks giant tortoises. Indeed he is an adept!
This one line is used to illustrate the Case.

"His contemporary the Elder of Kuan Hsi is worth laughing at." Haven't you heard—a monk asked Kuan Hsi, "I've long heard of Kuan Hsi ('Pouring Mountain Stream'). Now that I've come here I only see a hemp-soaking pool." Hsi said, "You just see the hemp-soaking pool; you don't see the pouring mountain stream." The monk said, "What is the pouring mountain stream?" Hsi said, "Swift as a whistling arrow."

Also a monk asked Huang Lung, "I've long heard of Huang Lung ('Yellow Dragon'), but now that I've come here I only see a red striped snake." Lung said, "You just see the red striped snake; you don't see the yellow dragon." The monk said, "What is the yellow dragon?" Lung said, "Slithering along." The monk said, "How is it when he suddenly encounters the (dragon-eating) Garuda bird?" Lung said, "Difficult to stay alive." The monk said, "If so, then he'll get eaten up by the bird." Lung said, "Thank you for feeding me."

These are both cases of setting up the solitary and dangerous. Though Kuan Hsi and Huang Lung are both right, nevertheless they did waste effort. They never equalled Chao Chou's ordinary action. That's why Hsueh Tou says, "Though he knew how to say 'Whistling Arrow,' his effort was in vain."

Leaving Kuan Hsi and Huang Lung aside for the moment, how will you understand when Chao Chou says, "It lets asses cross, it lets horses cross"? Try to do it.

Pai Chang's Wild Ducks

POINTER

The whole world does not hide it—his entire capacity stands alone revealed. He encounters situations without getting stuck—with every move he has the ability to assert himself. In his phrases there's no partiality—everywhere he has the intention to kill people.

But say, in the end, where do the Ancients go to rest? To test I'm citing this old case: look!

CASE

Once when Great Master Ma and Pai Chang were walking together they saw some wild ducks fly by.[1] The Great Master asked, "What is that?"[2] Chang said, "Wild ducks."[3] The Great Master said, "Where have they gone?"[4] Chang said, "They've flown away."[5] The Great Master then twisted Pai Chang's nose.[6] Chang cried out in pain.[7] The Great Master said, "When have they ever flown away?"[8]

NOTES

1. Two fellows in the weeds. They're rolling around in the weeds. Why suddenly notice the ducks?
2. You should know, Teacher. This old fellow doesn't even know his nostrils.
3. Chang's nostrils are already in the hands of the other man. He just offers the actual facts. The second ladleful of foul water will be even more poisonous.
4. His first arrow was still light, but the second arrow is deep. A second enticing peck. Here too Ma Tsu should know for himself.
5. He just rolls along behind Ma Tsu. He's stumbled past what's right in front of him.

357

6. The nostrils born of his parents are in the hands of someone else. Ma Tsu turned the spear around and twisted Chang's nostrils around.
7. It's right here. Can it be called wild ducks? Are you conscious of pain?
8. Better not deceive people. From the beginning this old fellow has been making his living inside a ghost cave.

COMMENTARY

If you observe this case with the correct eye, unexpectedly it's Pai Chang who has the correct basis, whereas Great Master Ma is creating waves where there is no wind. If all of you want to be teachers of Buddhas and Patriarchs, then study Pai Chang. If you want to be unable to save even yourselves, then study the Great Master Ma. Observe how those Ancients were never absent from Here, twenty-four hours a day.

At a young age Pai Chang left behind the dusts of wordly life and became well versed in the three studies (discipline, meditation, and wisdom). When Ma Tsu (known as) Ta Chi was teaching at Nan Ch'ang, Pai Chang set his heart on joining him. For twenty years he served as Ma Tsu's attendant, until the time of his second calling (on Ma Tsu, as related in the commentary to Case 11), when he was finally greatly enlightened at Ma Tsu's shout.

But these days some say, "Where there is fundamentally no enlightenment, they construct the gate of 'enlightenment' and establish this affair." If you view it in this way, you are like a flea on a lion's body feeding itself on the lion's flesh. Haven't you seen where an Ancient said, "If the source is not deep, the stream is not long; if the wisdom is not great, the vision is not far-reaching." If you entertain the understanding that enlightenment is a construct, how could the Buddhist Teaching have come down to the present?

Look: once when Great Master Ma and Pai Chang were walking together they saw some wild ducks fly by. How could the Great Master not have known they were wild ducks? Why did he nevertheless ask like this? Tell me, what does his meaning come down to? When Pai Chang merely followed up behind him, Ma Tsu then twisted his nose. Chang cried out in pain and Ma Tsu said, "When have they ever flown away?" At this Pai Chang had insight. But these days some people misunderstand: as soon as they're questioned, they immediately make a cry of pain. Fortunately they can't leap out of it.

When teachers of our school help people, they must make them penetrate through. You see that Pai Chang didn't understand, that he didn't avoid cutting his hand on the point. Ma Tsu just wanted to make him understand this matter. Thus it is said, "When you understand, you can make use of it wherever you are; if you don't understand, then the conventional truth prevails." If Ma Tsu hadn't twisted Pai Chang's nose at that time, the conventional truth would have prevailed. It's also necessary when encountering circumstances and meeting conditions to turn them around and return them to oneself; to have no gaps at any time is called "the ground of nature bright and clear." What's the use of one who just haunts the forests and fields, accepting what's ahead of an ass but behind a horse?[a]

Observe how Ma Tsu and Pai Chang act this way; though they seem radiant and spiritual, nevertheless they don't remain in radiance and spirituality. Pai Chang cried out in pain; if you see it as such, then the whole world does not hide it, and it is perfectly manifest everywhere. Thus it is said, "Penetrate one place, and you penetrate a thousand places, ten thousand places all at once."

When Ma Tsu went up to the hall the next day, as soon as the congregation had assembled, Pai Chang came forward and rolled up the bowing mat. Ma Tsu immediately left his seat. After he had returned to his abbot's quarters, he asked Pai Chang, "I had just gone up to the hall and had not yet preached; why did you roll up the mat right away?" Chang said, "Yesterday I had my nose twisted by you, Teacher, and it hurt." Tsu said, "Where were you keeping your mind yesterday?" Chang said, "Today the nose no longer hurts." Tsu said, "You have profound knowledge of Today's affair." Chang then bowed and returned to the attendants' quarters, crying. One of his fellow attendants asked, "Why are you crying?" Chang said, "Go ask our Master." The attendant then went to ask Ma Tsu. Tsu said, "Go ask Pai Chang." When the attendant returned to their quarters to ask Pai Chang, Chang laughed loudly. The attendant said, "You were just crying—now why are you laughing?"

Chang said, "I was crying before, now I'm laughing." Look at
Pai Chang after his enlightenment; turning smoothly, he can't
be trapped. Naturally he's sparkling clear on all sides.

VERSE

Wild ducks—
> Gathering in flocks. Here's another one.

Who knows where they are?
> Why use wild ducks? They're as numerous as hemp or
> millet seeds.

*Ma Tsu saw them coming and they had words with each
> other—*
> What end is there to creating complications? What did
> they say? Ma Tsu alone recognizes the outstanding one.

*He told all about the scene of the clouds on the mountains and
> the moon over the sea.*
> The ladle handle of the eastern house is long; the ladle
> handle of the western house is short. Who knows how
> many complications he created?

*As before Chang didn't understand, but said, "They've flown
> away."*
> Gaa! Don't say he didn't know how to speak. Where did
> they fly off to?

Pai Chang wanted to fly away,
> His nostrils were in the other man's hands. This is already
> adding footnotes for others.

But Ma Tsu held him fast.
> With grandmotherly kindness. What else did he say?

Speak! Speak!
> What is there to say? Don't make me speak too. Don't
> make a wild duck cry. Heavens! Right where you are you
> deserve thirty blows. Who knows where they went to?

COMMENTARY

Directly and immediately, Hsueh Tou makes his verse saying,
"Wild ducks—who knows where they are?" But say, how

many are there? "Ma Tsu saw them coming and they had
words with each other." This versifies Ma Tsu asking Pai
Chang, "What is that?" and Chang saying, "Wild ducks." "He
told all about the scene of the clouds on the mountains and the
moon over the sea." This versifies Ma Tsu again asking,
"Where have they gone?" The teaching which Great Master
Ma conveyed to Pai Chang spontaneously revealed everything.
As before Chang did not understand; instead he said, "They've
flown away." Twice he missed it.

   With "Pai Chang wanted to fly away, but Ma Tsu held him
fast," Hsueh Tou settles the case on the basis of the facts. He
also says, "Speak! Speak!" This is where Hsueh Tou turns
himself around. But say, how will you speak? If you make a cry
of pain, then you're wrong. If you don't make a cry of pain, then
how do you understand it? Though Hsueh Tou versifies most
wondrously, no matter what he does he can't leap out either.

TRANSLATORS' NOTES

a.   "What's ahead of an ass but behind a horse" is often referred
     specifically to the "radiant spirituality," a designation of the con-
     scious radiance of the mind temporarily cleared or halted by
     meditation, which is beyond unregenerate ignorant people, but is
     not yet thorough realization of personal and phenomenal empti-
     ness, still in the realm of subjectivity.

Yun Men Extends Both Hands

POINTER

Having penetrated through and out of birth and death, he sets his devices in motion. Perfectly at ease, he shears through iron and cuts through nails. Wherever he goes he covers heaven and covers earth.

But say, whose behavior is this? To test I'm citing this old case; look!

CASE

Yun Men asked a monk, "Where did you come here from?"[1] The monk said, "Hsi Ch'an."[2] Yun Men said, "What words and phrases are there at Hsi Ch'an these days?"[3] The monk extended both hands;[4] Yun Men slapped him once.[5]

The monk said, "I'm still talking."[6] Yun Men then extended his two hands.[7] The monk was speechless,[8] so Yun Men hit him.[9]

NOTES

1. Don't say Hsi Ch'an. A probing pole, a reed shade. Don't say east, west, north or south.
2. As it turns out, he's too literal. At that moment the monk should have given him some of his own provisions.
3. "I want to bring it up, but I fear that it would startle you, Teacher." Yun Men profoundly discriminates among oncoming winds. "Hsi Ch'an was like you, Teacher, talking in your sleep."
4. He's been defeated. He took in a thief and got his house ransacked. This will inevitably cause people to doubt.
5. He acts according to the imperative. The monk should be hit. A fleeting chance is hard to meet with.
6. So you want to change your plea? Nevertheless, he seems to have the ability to capture the flag and carry off the drums.

7. Danger! The monk is being given an excellent mount, but he doesn't know how to ride it.
8. What a pity!
9. Don't let him go. It should be Yun Men who takes this beating. Why? When you don't settle what should be settled, instead you invite disorder. How many blows should you receive? Yun Men let up on him a little. If he hadn't let up, what should he have done?

COMMENTARY

Yun Men asked this monk, "Where did you come here from?" The monk said, "Hsi Ch'an." This is direct face to face talk, like a flash of lightening. Men said, "What words and phrases are there at Hsi Ch'an these days?" This too is just ordinary conversation. This monk, however, is also an adept; contrary to expectations, he goes to test Yun Men—he immediately extended his two hands. If it had been an ordinary person who met with this test, we would have seen him flustered and agitated. But Yun Men has a mind like flint struck sparks, like flashing lightening; immediately he slapped him.

The monk said, "You may hit me all right, but nevertheless I'm still talking." This monk had a place to turn around, so Yun Men opened up and extended his two hands. The monk was speechless, so Yun Men hit him.

Look—since Yun Men is an adept, whenever he takes a step he knows where the step comes down. He knows how to observe in front and take notice behind, not losing his way. This monk only knows how to look ahead; he's unable to observe behind.

VERSE

At once he takes the tiger's head and the tiger's tail—
    The single-edged sword that kills people, the double-edged sword that brings people to life. Only this monk can handle it. A thousand soldiers are easy to get, but one general is hard to find.

His stern majesty extends everywhere.
    He cuts off the tongues of everyone on earth. He covers
    heaven and covers earth.

I ask back, "Didn't you know how dangerous it was?"
    You shouldn't blindly fetter and beat them. From the be-
    ginning Hsueh Tou himself didn't know. You are speak-
    ing carelessly, Reverend.

Hsueh Tou says, "I leave off."
    If he hadn't left off, then what? Everyone on earth loses
    out all at once. I hit the meditation seat once.

COMMENTARY

Hsueh Tou's verse on this story is very easy to understand—its
overall meaning is to praise the sharp point of Yun Men's ability. Thus he says, "At once he takes the tiger's head and the
tiger's tail." An Ancient said, "Occupy the tiger's head, take
the tiger's tail, then at the first phrase you'll understand the
source meaning." Hsueh Tou just settles the case on the basis
of the facts. He likes the way Yun Men is able to occupy the
tiger's head and also take the tiger's tail. When the monk extended his two hands and Yun Men immediately hit him, this
was occupying the tiger's head. When Yun Men extended two
hands and the monk was speechless so that Yun Men hit him
again, this was taking the tiger's tail. When head and tail are
taken together, the eye is like a shooting star.

Yun Men is naturally like stone-struck sparks, like flashing
lightning; in fact, "His stern majesty extends everywhere."
The wind whistles all over the world.

"I ask back, 'Didn't you know how dangerous it was?'" Unavoidably there was danger. Hsueh Tou says, "I leave off." But
say, right now as I don't leave off, what will you do? Everyone
in the world will have to take a beating.

Followers of Ch'an these days all say that when Yun Men
extended his two hands, the monk should have repaid him
with some of his own provisions. This seems correct, but in
reality isn't. Yun Men can't just get you to stop this way—
there must be something else besides.

Tao Wu's Condolence Call

POINTER

Secure and intimate with the whole of reality, one obtains realization right there. In contact with the flow, able to turn things around, one assumes responsibility directly.

As for cutting off confusion in the light of a stone-struck spark or a flash of lightning, or towering up like a mile-high wall where one occupies the tiger's head and takes the tiger's tail—this I leave aside for the moment. Is there a way to help people by letting out a continuous path or not? To test, I cite this: look!

CASE

Tao Wu and Chien Yuan went to a house to make a condolence call. Yuan hit the coffin and said, "Alive or dead?"[1] Wu said, "I won't say alive, and I won't say dead."[2] Yuan said, "Why won't you say?"[3] Wu said, "I won't say."[4] Halfway back, as they were returning,[5] Yuan said, "Tell me right away, Teacher; if you don't tell me, I'll hit you."[6] Wu said, "You may hit me, but I won't say,"[7] Yuan then hit him.[8]

Later Tao Wu passed on. Yuan went to Shih Shuang and brought up the foregoing story.[9] Shuang said, "I won't say alive, and I won't say dead."[10] Yuan said, "Why won't you say?"[11] Shuang said, "I won't say, I won't say."[12] At these words Yuan had an insight."[13]

One day Yuan took a hoe into the teaching hall and crossed back and forth, from east to west and west to east.[14] Shuang said, "What are you doing?"[15] Yuan said, "I'm looking for relics of our late master."[16] Shuang said, "Vast waves spread far and wide, foaming billows flood the skies—what relics of our late master are you looking for?"[17]

Hsueh Tou added a comment saying, "Heavens! Heavens!"[18]

Yuan said, "This is just where I should apply effort."[19]
Fu of T'ai Yuan said, "The late master's relics are still present."[20]

NOTES

1. What is he saying? He sure isn't alert. This fellow is still lingering in duality.
2. When a dragon puffs, fog gathers; when a tiger roars, wind rises. He buys the hat to fit the head. He's kind-hearted.
3. He's stumbled past. As it turns out, he misunderstands.
4. He pours foul water right on Yuan's head. The first arrow was still light, but the second arrow goes deep.
5. Not very alert.
6. If he hits, then he'll be getting somewhere. It's rare to meet with the pierced-ear traveller (Bodhidharma); you often encounter travellers who cut a notch in the boat (thinking to mark the spot on the water which the boat is going over at a given time).[a] If you are like this latter kind of fool, you'll enter hell as fast as an arrow.
7. Again and again he must repeat this. He gets in close to take him. This old fellow's whole body is covered with muddy water. His original attitude is unchanging.
8. He should be hit. But say, why does he hit him? From the beginning there have been people who have received unjust beatings.
9. He knows, yet deliberately offends. He doesn't know whether he's right or wrong—if he's right, that would be wonderful.
10. How fresh and new! Yet there have always been people who eat this kind of food and drink.
11. Though his words are the same, his intent is different. But say, is this the same as or different from his asking before?
12. In the heavens and on earth. If the waves of Ts'ao Ch'i resembled each other, innumerable ordinary people would get bogged down.
13. The blind man! Better not fool me.
14. Within death he has found life. He should show some life for his late master. Don't question him—but observe this fellow's embarrassment.
15. He just follows along behind.
16. He hangs a medicine bag on the back of a hearse. Too bad that he was not so careful at first. What are you saying, Yuan?
17. Only that adept could do this. Why gather in crowds?

18. Too late. Hsueh Tou draws his bow after the thief has gone. He should be buried in the same pit.
19. But tell me, what does this really mean? What has the late master ever said to you? From beginning to end, and even up till now, this fellow has been unable to get himself out.
20. Does everyone see them? They're like flashing lightning. What worn out straw sandals are these? Fu has realized a little bit.

COMMENTARY

Tao Wu and Chien Yuan went to a house to make a condolence call. Yuan hit the coffin and said, "Alive or dead?" Wu said, "I won't say alive, and I won't say dead." If you can immediately enter at these lines, if at these words you immediately know what they come down to, then this is the key to penetrating beyond life and death. Otherwise, if you can't, then you will miss it over and over again even though it's right in front of you.

Observe how these Ancients, whether walking, standing, sitting, or lying down, were always mindful of this matter. As soon as they got to the house to offer condolences, Chien Yuan hit the coffin and asked Tao Wu, "Alive or dead?" Without stirring a hairsbreadth, Tao Wu answered him saying, "I won't say alive, and I won't say dead." Chien Yuan was face to face with it, but he stumbled past, running after the other man's words. He went on to say, "Why won't you say?" Wu said, "I won't say, I won't say." This can be called Wu meeting an error with an error, his heart bared entirely.

Yuan was still not awake himself: halfway back as they were returning he again said, "Tell me right away, Teacher; if you don't tell me, I'll hit you." What does this fellow know of good and bad? This is what is called "a good intention not getting a good reward." With tender kindness as before, Tao Wu said more to him; "You may hit me, but I won't say." Yuan then hit him. Even so, Tao Wu nevertheless won the point. Tao Wu was dripping with blood like this to help him, but Chien Yuan could be so unseeing!

After being hit, Tao Wu then said to Chien Yuan, "You should go away for a while. I fear that if the monastery's director of affairs finds out, he would make trouble for you." He secretly sent Chien Yuan away. Yuan later came to a small temple where he heard a workman reciting the Avalokitesvara scripture, where it says, "To those who would attain salvation as monks, he appears as a monk to expound the Dharma for them." Suddenly Yuan was greatly enlightened and said, "At that time I was wrongly suspicious of my late teacher. How was I to know that this affair isn't in words and phrases?" As an Ancient said, "Even someone great beyond measure can be whirled around in the stream of words."

Some interpret intellectually and say that when Tao Wu said, "I won't say, I won't say," he had thereby already said something, that this is what is called "turning a back-flip, making people unable to get ahold of you." If you understand in this fashion, how will you attain tranquility? If your feet tread the real earth, you aren't even a hairsbreadth away.

Haven't you heard? Seven women sages were travelling through the Forest of Corpses. One of the women pointed to a corpse and asked her sisters, "The corpse is here—where is the person?" The eldest sister said, "What? What?" and all seven together experienced the tolerance of birthlessness. But say, how many are there like this? In a thousand or ten thousand, there's just one.

Later Chien Yuan went to Shih Shuang and related his previous conversation with Tao Wu. Same as before, Shih Shuang said, "I won't say alive, and I won't say dead," and Yuan said, "Why won't you say?" When Shih Shuang said, "I won't say, I won't say," Yuan was immediately enlightened.

One day Yuan took a hoe into the teaching hall and crossed back and forth, from east to west and west to east. He intended to display his insight. Sure enough Shuang asked him, "What are you doing?" Yuan said, "I'm looking for relics of our late master." Shuang then cut off his footsteps, saying, "Vast waves spread far and wide, foaming billows flood the skies—what relics of our late master are you looking for?" Since Yuan was looking for relics of the late master, why did Shih Shuang nevertheless talk to him this way? At this point, if you can comprehend the words, "I won't say alive, and I won't say dead," then you will know that from beginning to end the entire capacity is put to use. If you make up rationalizations, hesitate and ponder, then it will be impossible to see.

Chien Yuan said, "This is just where I should apply effort."

See how after his enlightenment he can speak spontaneously so extraordinarily.

Tao Wu's skull bone was golden-hued; when struck it sounded like metal.

Hsueh Tou commented, "Heavens! Heavens!" His meaning comes down on both sides.

Fu of T'ai Yuan said, "The late master's relics are still present." Naturally what he said was fitting—at once he put this loose end in place.

But tell me, what is the most essential place? How is effort applied? Haven't you heard it said that if you penetrate in one place you penetrate in a thousand, ten-thousand places all at once." If you can penetrate "I won't say, I won't say," then you cut off the tongues of everyone on earth. If you can't penetrate this, then you must study for yourself and awaken yourself. You mustn't take it easy and let the days go by—you must value the time.

VERSE

Rabbits and horses have horns—
> Chop them off. How extraordinary! How fresh and new!

Oxen and Rams have no horns.
> Chop them off. What pattern is being formed? You may fool others.

Nary a hair, nary a wisp—
> "In the heavens and on earth, I alone am the honored one." Where will you search?

Like mountains, like peaks.
> Where are they? Waves arising on level ground clog your nostrils.

The golden relics still exist right now—
> Cutting off tongues, blocking throats. I put them to one side; I only fear that there won't be anyone who can recognize them.

With white foaming waves flooding the skies, where can they be put?
> Hsueh Tou lets his move go. They're right under your feet but you miss them. They can't be put in your eyes or ears.

There's no place to put them—
   After all. Yet Hsueh Tou has managed somewhat. But as
   it turns out he's sunk in a deep pit.
*Even the one who returned to the West with one shoe has lost
   them.*[b]
   If the ancestral shrine is not completed, the trouble extends to the descendants. I'll hit, saying, "Then why are
   they here?"

COMMENTARY

Hsueh Tou understands how to add footnotes exceptionally
well. He is a descendant of Yun Men, with the hammer and
tongs to have three phrases present in every single phrase.
Where it's hard to express, he explains thoroughly; the un-
openable he opens up. He goes to the most crucial and essential
place and produces it in verse, immediately saying, "Rabbits
and horses have horns—oxen and rams have no horns." Tell
me, why do rabbits and horses have horns? Why then do oxen
and rams have no horns? Only if you can penetrate the preceding story (in the case) will you realize that Hsueh Tou has a
way to help people.
   Some mistakenly say, "Not saying is saying; having no
phrases is having phrases. Though rabbits and horses have no
horns, yet Hsueh Tou says they have horns. Though oxen and
rams have horns, nevertheless Hsueh Tou says they don't." But
this has nothing to do with it. They are far from knowing that
the Ancient's thousand changes and ten thousand transformations, which manifest such supernatural powers, were just to
break up the ghost cave of your spirit. If you can penetrate
through, it's not even worth using the word "understand."

   Rabbits and horses have horns—
   Oxen and rams have no horns.
   Nary a hair, nary a wisp—
   Like mountains, like peaks.

These four lines are like the wish-fulfilling jewel. Hsueh Tou
has spit it out whole right in front of you.
   The last part of the verse is all settling the case according to
the facts. "The golden relics still exist right now—with white

foamy waves flooding the skies, where can they be put?" This versifies the statements of Shih Shuang and Fu of T'ai Yuan. Why is there no place to put them? "Even the one who returned to the West with one shoe has lost them." The sacred tortoise is dragging his tail—this is where Hsueh Tou turns around to help people. An Ancient said, "He just studies the living phrase; he doesn't study the dead phrase." Since the relics are lost, why is that bunch still struggling with each other over them?

TRANSLATORS' NOTES

a. Once someone riding in a boat happened to drop his sword overboard; he marked the spot on the boat, but as it is also said in reference to this story, "the sword was long gone."

b. After Bodhidharma was supposed to have died and been interred, he was allegedly seen walking back to India with one shoe in hand. When his coffin was exhumed, nothing but a single shoe was found inside. Hence this refers to Bodhidharma, the first patriarch of Ch'an in China.

Ch'in Shan's One Arrowpoint
Smashes Three Barriers

POINTER

The Buddhas never appeared in the world—there is nothing to be given to people. The Patriarch never came from the West—he never passed on the transmission by mind. Since people of these times do not understand, they frantically search outside themselves. They are far from knowing that the One Great Matter right where they are cannot be grasped even by a thousand sages.

Right now, where do seeing and not seeing, hearing and not hearing, speaking and not speaking, knowing and not knowing come from? If you are unable to apprehend clearly, then try to understand inside the cave of entangling vines.[a] To test, I cite this: look!

CASE

Ch'an traveller Liang asked Ch'in Shan, "How is it when a single arrowhead smashes three barriers?"[1]

Shan said, "Bring out the lord within the barriers for me to see."[2]

Liang said, "So then knowing my fault I must change."[3]

Shan said, "Why wait any longer?"[4]

Liang said, "A well-shot arrow doesn't hit anywhere," and (started to) leave.[5] Shan said, "Come here a minute."[6] Liang turned his head;[7] Shan held him tight and said, "Leaving aside for the moment a single arrowhead smashing three barriers, let's see you shoot an arrow."[8] Liang hesitated,[9] so Shan hit him seven times and said, "I'll allow as this fellow will be doubting for thirty more years."[10]

NOTES

1. Danger! Undeniably Liang is extraordinary—he is a fierce general.
2. He comes on directly. He wants everyone to know; Mt. Chu is high, Mt. An is low.
3. He sees his opportunity and acts. He's already fallen into the secondary.
4. There's capture, there's release. When the wind moves the grass bends.
5. After all. So Liang is trying to change his plea. He strikes his second blow, but Ch'in Shan feels no pain.
6. Summoning him is easy, dispatching him is hard. What good is someone who turns his head when called?
7. As it turns out Liang couldn't hold fast. He's hit.
8. Ch'in Shan lies down in the tiger's mouth. Waves against the current. Having seen one's duty but not doing it is lack of courage.
9. As it turns out, he searches without finding. I'll hit, saying, "Too bad."
10. The imperative must be so. There's a beginning, there's an end. Ch'in Shan is correct at the beginning and correct at the end. It's Ch'in Shan who should receive this beating.

COMMENTARY

Ch'an traveller Liang was undeniably a battle-tested general. In Ch'in Shan's hand he turned to the left and revolved to the right, bringing down his whip and flashing his stirrups. In the end, what a pity—his bow is broken, and his arrows are used up. Even so, "General Li Kuang, though he had a glorious reputation, was never enfeoffed as a noble, so it was useless."

This public case has one exit and one entry, one capture and one release. "Taking charge of the situation, he brings it up face to face; face to face, taking charge of the situation is swift." Throughout there is no falling into existence and nonexistence or gain and loss. This is called "mysterious activity." If one lacks strength, then he will stumble.

This monk too was a brave and spirited patchrobed one; he posed a question that really startles the crowd. Being an expert teacher of our school, Ch'in Shan immediately knew where his question came down. How is it when a single arrowhead smashes the three barriers? Ch'in Shan's reply meant, "For the moment leave aside your shooting through; try to bring out the lord within the barriers for me to see." Liang's saying, "So then knowing my fault I must change," was undeniably extraordinary. Ch'in Shan said, "Why wait any longer?" See how he replied—this question of Ch'in Shan's has no gaps.

Finally Ch'an traveller Liang just said, "A well-shot arrow doesn't hit anywhere." He shook out his sleeves to go away. As soon as he saw him talking this way, Ch'in Shan immediately called out to him, "Come here a minute, Reverend."[b] As it turned out Liang couldn't hold fast; he turned his head back then. Ch'in Shan held him tight and said, "Leaving aside for the moment a single arrowhead smashing three barriers, let's see you shoot an arrow." When Liang hesitated, Ch'in Shan immediately struck him seven blows. After this he went on to pronounce a curse on Liang saying, "I'll allow this fellow will be doubting for thirty more years."

Followers of Ch'an these days all say, "Why didn't he hit him eight times or six times? Why just seven times? Or else why didn't he hit him immediately as he was asking him to try to shoot an arrow?" Though this seems right, in reality it isn't. For this case you must not cherish the least bit of rational calculation in your heart; you must pass beyond the words. Only then will you be able to have a way to smash the three barriers[c] at a single phrase and to shoot an arrow. If you keep thinking of right and wrong, you will never be able to get a grasp on it.

At that time, if this monk had been a real man, Ch'in Shan would have been in great danger too. Since Liang could not carry out the imperative, he couldn't avoid it being carried out on him. But say, after all, who is the lord within the barriers? Look at Hsueh Tou's verse:

VERSE

I bring out the lord within the barriers for you—
    On target. Face to face, still you miss it. Retreat! Retreat!

You disciples who would shoot an arrow, don't be careless!
  Once dead, one doesn't come back to life again. Very
  obscure. Gone by.

Take an eye and the ears go deaf;
  In the left eye half a pound. Hsueh Tou lets his move go.
  On the left not advancing, on the right not retreating.

Let go an ear and the eyes both go blind.
  In the right eye eight ounces. There's only one road. Advance and you fall into a pit; retreat and a ferocious tiger
  will bite your leg.

I can admire a single arrowpoint smashing three barriers—
  How is it when the entire capacity comes forth this way?
  What is he saying? The barriers have been smashed, the
  barriers have fallen.

The trail of the arrow is truly clear.
  Dead man! Bah! I'll hit, saying, "Do you see it?"

You don't see!
  A leper drags along his companions. He's creating complications.

Hsuan Sha had words for this:
  Who isn't Hsuan Sha?

"A great adept is the primordial ancestor of mind."
  With one line he cuts off the flow and puts myriad
  impulses to rest. The nostrils of the great adept are in my
  hands. Before heaven and earth and the world existed,
  where would you rest your body and establish your life?

COMMENTARY

Several of the lines of this verse draw on the words of a verse of
Kuei Tsung. Since Kuei Tsung made up this verse in the old
days, he was given the name Kuei Tsung ('return to the
source'). Within the gate of our school this is called "talk of the
source meaning."

Later Tung An heard of this case and said, "Mr. Liang was
well able to shoot arrows, but in essence he didn't know how to

hit the target." There was a monk then who asked, "How can one hit the target?" An said, "Who is the lord within the barriers?" Later there was a monk who cited this to Ch'in Shan. Shan said, "Even if Mr. Liang had been this way, he still wouldn't have avoided Ch'in Shan's mouth. Although this is so, T'ung An is not good-hearted."

Hsueh Tou says, "I bring out the lord within the barriers for you." Open your eyes and you can see, close your eyes and you can see too. With form, without form—all is cut into three sections. "You disciples who would shoot an arrow, don't be careless." If you are able to shoot well, you won't be careless. If you don't shoot well, then it's obvious that you are careless.

"Take an eye and the ears go deaf; let go an ear and the eyes both go blind." Tell me, when an eye is taken, why is it nevertheless the ears that go deaf? When an ear is let go, why then is it the eyes that both go blind? You can penetrate these words only if you have no grasping or rejection; if you are grasping and rejecting, then it will be impossible to see.

"I can admire a single arrowpoint smashing three barriers— the trail of the arrow is truly clear." Ch'an traveller Liang asked, "How is it when a single arrowpoint smashes the three barriers?" and Ch'in Shan said, "Bring out the lord within the barriers for me to see." These statements and everything down to T'ung An's case at the end are all "the trail of the arrow." In the end, what is it?"

"You don't see? Hsuan Sha had words for this: 'A great adept is the primordial ancestor of mind.'" It is commonplace to take mind as the ultimate principle of the school of the Patriarchs; here though, why is the great adept still the ancestor of this mind even before heaven and earth were born? If you can thoroughly understand this time and season, only then will you be able to recognize the lord within the barriers.

"The trail of the arrow is truly clear." If you want to hit the target, there clearly is a trail behind the arrow. But say, what is the trail behind the arrow? Before you'll understand, you must apply concentrated mental effort on your own.

"A great adept is the primordial ancestor of mind." Hsuan Sha often taught his community with these words. This is from a verse of Kuei Tsung's which Hsueh Tou has wrongly attributed to Hsuan Sha. Students of today who take this mind as the ancestral source can study until Maitreya Buddha comes down to be born here and still never understand. For one who is a great adept, even mind is still just the descendant.

"Heaven and earth not yet distinct" is already the secondary. Tell me, at just such a time, what is "before heaven and earth"?

TRANSLATORS' NOTES

a. Tangled or entangling vines is an expression colloquially meaning complications, and has been so translated. In Ch'an talk it is often used on one level to refer specifically to words, hence the public cases (*kung an*) themselves.

b. "Reverend" used here was used sometimes by Ch'an teachers as a term of direct address, hence is not always necessary to translate, except for emphasis. In formal usage it really means teacher, so it is possible that there can be some irony in the Ch'an usage. The original Sanskrit word, *Acarya*, was transliterated into Chinese syllables instead of semantic translation; the connotations of teacher, exemplar, and guide tended in common usage to fade into a general term of respect.

c. Nothing is specifically said about what the three barriers are; since the point seems to be the lord within the barriers, perhaps it is pointless to say anything. The form of Liang's question need not be considered totally arbitrary, however; we have seen mention, for example, of Yun Men's three phrases within a phrase, cutting off the stream, covering heaven and earth, and going along with the waves. Pai Chang said that the Buddhist Teachings all had three phases (expressed verbally and metaphorically as phrases): detachment from everything, not abiding in detachment (not seeing that there is anything really real to either grasp or reject), and not having any understanding of non-abiding (no awareness of knowledge of non-duality as such, no more delusion of subtle and extremely subtle knowledge). In the Lin Chi Ch'an school of the Southern Sung dynasty, after Yuan Wu, when the use of *kung an* as meditation themes was popular, there also was reference to three phases of "understanding" a *kung an*; seeing its intent, practical application, and transcendance. All of these designated states of attainment could be called "barriers"; probably "three barriers" means all barriers.

Chao Chou's Stupid Oaf

POINTER

Before you have penetrated, it all seems like a silver mountain, like an iron wall. When you have been able to penetrate, from the beginning it was your self that was the silver mountain, the iron wall.

If someone asks me, "So what?" I would just say to him, "Here, if you can reveal an action and observe an environment, occupy the essential bridge without letting profane or holy pass, this would not be beyond your inherent capacity."

If, on the other hand, you are not yet thus, observe the look of an Ancient.

CASE

A monk asked Chao Chou, " 'The Ultimate Path has no difficulties—just avoid picking and choosing.' What is not picking and choosing?"[1]

Chou said, " 'In the heavens and on earth I alone am the Honored One.' "[2]

The monk said, "This is still picking and choosing."[3]

Chou said, "Stupid oaf! Where is the picking and choosing?"[4] The monk was speechless.[5]

NOTES

1. So many people cannot swallow these iron brambles. There are many people who have doubts about this. His whole mouth is filled with frost.
2. He heaps up a pile of bones on level ground. All at once he has pierced the nostrils of patchrobed monks. A talisman hard as cast iron.

378

3. As it turns out he's rolled along after Chao Chou. He challenges this old fellow.
4. Mountains crumble, rocks shatter.
5. I forgive you thirty blows. His eyes open wide, his mouth is agape.

COMMENTARY

The monk questioned Chao Chou about (the saying) "The Ultimate Path has no difficulties—just avoid picking and choosing." The Third Patriarch's *Inscription of the Believing Heart* starts off directly with these two lines. There are quite a few people who misunderstand. How so? (According to them,) the Ultimate Path is fundamentally without difficulties, but also without anything that's not difficult; it's just that it's only adverse to picking and choosing. If you understand in this fashion, in ten thousand years you won't even see it in dreams.

Chao Chou often used this saying to question people. This monk reversed this by taking this saying to question him. If you look to the words, then this monk does after all startle heaven and shake the earth. If it is not in the words, then what? You must be able to turn this little key before it will open. To grab the tiger's whiskers, you must be able to do it on your own abilities. Heedless of the mortal danger, this monk dared to grab the tiger's whiskers, so he said, "This is still picking and choosing." Chao Chou immediately blocked off his mouth by saying, "Stupid oaf! Where is the picking and choosing?" If the monk had asked someone else, he would have seen him flustered and confused. But what could he do about this old fellow who was an adept? Chao Chou moved where it was impossible to move, turned around where it was impossible to turn around.

If you can penetrate all evil and poisonous words and phrases, even down to a thousand differences and ten thousand forms, then all conventional fabrications will be the excellent flavor of purified ghee. If you can get to where you touch reality, then you will see Chao Chou's naked heart in its entirety.

"Stupid oaf" is a country expression of the people of Fu Chou, to revile people for being without intelligence. When the monk said, "This is still picking and choosing," Chao Chou said, "Stupid oaf! Where is the picking and choosing?" The eye

of teachers of our school must be thus, like the golden winged
Garuda bird parting the ocean waters to seize a dragon directly
and swallow it.

VERSE

Deep as the ocean,
>What measure is this? The abyssal source is impossible to
>fathom. This still hasn't got a half of it.

Firm as a mountain.
>Who can shake him? This is still only halfway there.

A mosquito sports in the fierce wind of the sky,
>There are others like this. After all, he didn't assess his
>strength; he certainly didn't measure himself.

An ant tries to shake an iron pillar.
>There's no different dirt in the same hole. He's out of
>touch. You're a fellow student with him.

Picking, choosing—
>Carrying water to sell at the river. What is he saying?
>Chao Chou has come.

A cloth drum under the eaves.[a]
>It is already present before any words. They're buried in
>the same pit, as numerous as hemp and millet seeds. I hit,
>saying, "I'll block off your throats."

COMMENTARY

Hsueh Tou explains Chao Chou's two lines in the case by
saying, "Deep as the ocean, firm as a mountain." The monk
said, "This is still picking and choosing," so Hsueh Tou says
that this monk is just like a mosquito playing in a gale, like an
ant trying to shake an iron pillar. Hsueh Tou praises this
monk's great bravery. Why? This "the ultimate path has no
difficulties" is something superior people use, yet this monk
dared to talk in this way. Chao Chou did not let him go; he
immediately said, "Stupid oaf! Where is the picking and choosing?" Isn't this a fierce wind, an iron pillar?

"Picking, choosing—a cloth drum hung under the eaves."
At the end Hsueh Tou picks this up to bring you to life. If you
recognize it clearly, then you are carrying the whole thing
yourself. What's the reason? Haven't you heard it said that if
you want to attain intimate understanding, don't use a question to ask. That is why "the cloth drum under the eaves".

TRANSLATORS' NOTES

a. A cloth drum makes no sound when beaten; just so, Tenkei ex-
    plains, asking questions ('beating the drum') will never yield the
    real answer. Ultimately all discrimination, even between dis-
    crimination and clarity, is beating a cloth drum; the sound disap-
    pears in the emptiness of space.

Chao Chou Can't Explain

CASE

A monk asked Chao Chou, " 'The Ultimate Path has no difficulties—just avoid picking and choosing'—isn't this a cliché for people of these times?"[1]

Chou said, "Once someone asked me, and I really couldn't explain for five years."[2]

NOTES

1. A double case. This too is a point which makes people doubt. Treading on a scale beam, hard as iron. There's still this one. Don't judge others on the basis of yourself.
2. Honest speech is better than a red face. A monkey eats a caterpillar, a mosquito bites an iron ox.

COMMENTARY

Chao Chou usually didn't use blows or shouts; his action went beyond blows and shouts. This monk's question was also very special; it would have been hard for anyone but Chao Chou to answer him. Since Chao Chou was an adept, he just said to him, "Once someone asked me, and I really couldn't explain for five years." The question towered up like a mile-high wall, and the answer didn't make light of it. Just understand it this way and it's right here. If you don't understand, then don't make rational calculations.

Haven't you heard how when the man of the Path Tsung of T'ou Tzu was the scribe in Hsueh Tou's community, Hsueh Tou had him immerse himself in "The Ultimate Path has no difficulties; just avoid picking and choosing." Thereby Tsung had an awakening. One day Hsueh Tou asked him, "What is

382

the meaning of 'The Ultimate Path has no difficulties; just avoid picking and choosing'?" Tsung said, "Animal, animal." Later he dwelt in seclusion on Mt. T'ou Tzu. Whenever he went to serve as an abbot, he wrapped his straw sandals and his scriptural texts in his robe. A monk asked him "What is your family style, Wayfarer?" Tsung said, "Straw sandals wrapped in a robe." The monk said, "What does this mean?" Tsung said, "T'ung Ch'eng (the neighboring city) is under my bare feet."

Thus it is said, "Making offerings to the Buddha is not a matter of a lot of incense." If you can penetrate through and escape, then letting go or holding on rest with oneself. Since this case is one question and one answer, clear and perfectly obvious, why then did Chao Chou say that he couldn't explain? But tell me, is this a cliché for people of these times or not? Did Chao Chou answer him inside or outside the nest of cliché.[a] You must realize that this matter isn't in words and phrases. If there's a fellow who penetrates the bone and penetrates the marrow, whose faith is thoroughgoing, then he's like a dragon reaching the water, like a tiger taking to the mountains.

VERSE

The Elephant King trumpets
  Noblest of the noble, richest of the rich. Who isn't awed? Good news.
The Lion roars.
  An expert among experts. The hundred beasts' brains burst. A good route to enter by.
Flavorless talk
  When we're reviling each other, I'll let you lock jaws with me. It's like an iron spike; what place is there to bite into? He couldn't explain for five years and more; carrying all China in a single-leaf boat, far in the distant flats, waves are rising; who knows that there is yet another, better realm of thought?
Blocks off people's mouths.
  When we're spitting on each other, I'll let you spray me with slobber. Ha! What are you saying, Reverend?

South, north, east, west—
    Is there? Is there? In the heavens and on earth. Heavens!
    Heavens!
The raven flies, the rabbit runs.
    From past and from present. Buried alive all at once.

COMMENTARY

Chao Chou said, "Once someone asked me, and I really couldn't explain for five years." This is like "The Elephant King trumpets, the Lion roars. Flavorless talk blocks off people's mouths. South, north, east, west—the raven flies, the rabbit runs." If Hsueh Tou didn't have the last word, where else would he have come from? Since "the raven flies, the rabbit runs,"[b] tell me, where do Chao Chou, Hsueh Tou, and I end up?

TRANSLATORS' NOTES

a. In literary Chinese, the word 'nest' is used to refer to a cliché; that is, something people stick to. It is used in the same way in Ch'an to refer to words and sayings which have become cliché, and generally to any rut or habit in which one 'nests' complacently, any point on which one depends.
b. The raven and rabbit also refer to the sun and moon; their flight is the passage of terrestrial time.

Chao Chou's Why Not Quote It Fully?

POINTER

He includes the heavens and encompasses the earth, going beyond holy and profane. On the tips of the hundred weeds he points out the wondrous mind of nirvana; within the forest of shields and spears he decisively establishes the lifeline of patchrobed monks.

But tell me, endowed with whose power, can one get to be this way? As a test I cite this: look!

CASE

A monk asked Chao Chou, " 'The Ultimate Path has no difficulties—just avoid picking and choosing.[1] As soon as there are words and speech, this is picking and choosing.'[2] So how do you help people, Teacher?"[3]

Chou said, "Why don't you quote this saying in full?"[4] The monk said, "I only remember up to here."[5]

Chou said, "It's just this: 'This Ultimate Path has no difficulties—just avoid picking and choosing.' "[6]

NOTES

1. Again it's hauled out. What is he saying?
2. He takes a mouthful of frost.
3. He presses this old fellow. Gaa!
4. The thief is a small man, but his wisdom surpasses a lord's. Chao Chou is a thief who steals in broad daylight. He's riding the thief's horse in pursuit of the thief.
5. Two fellows playing with a mud ball. The monk has encountered a thief. When immobile it's hard to be a worthy opponent for Chao Chou.

6. In the end it's up to this old fellow. The monk has his eyes snatched away; he's been overtaken.

COMMENTARY

Chao Chou saying, "It's just this: 'The Ultimate Path has no difficulties—just avoid picking and choosing,' " is like a stone-struck spark, like a flash of lightning. Capturing and releasing, killing and giving life—he has such independent mastery. All over they said that Chao Chou had eloquence beyond the common crowd.

Chao Chou often taught his community with this speech, saying, "The Ultimate Path has no difficulties—just avoid picking and choosing. As soon as there are words and speech, 'this is picking and choosing,' 'this is clarity.' This old monk does not abide within clarity; do you still preserve anything or not?" Once there was a monk who asked, "Since you do not abide in clarity, what is to be preserved?" Chou said, "I don't know either." The monk said, "Since you don't know, Teacher, why do you say you don't abide in clarity?" Chou said, "It's enough just to ask about this matter. Now bow and withdraw."

Later a monk picked on his gap and went to question him; this monk's questioning was undeniably extraordinary, but nevertheless it was just mental activity. Someone other than Chao Chou would have been unable to handle this monk. But what could he do? Chao Chou was an adept and immediately said, "Why don't you quote this saying in full?"

This monk too understood how to turn himself around and show his mettle; he said, "I only remember up to here." It seems just like an arrangement. Directly after the monk spoke, Chao Chou immediately answered him; he didn't need any calculations. An Ancient said of this, "Continuity is indeed very difficult." Chao Chou distinguished dragons from snakes and differentiated right from wrong; this goes back to his being an adept in his own right. Chao Chou snatched this monk's eyes away without running afoul of his sharp point. Without relying on calculations, he was spontaneously exactly appropriate.

It's wrong to say either that he had words or didn't have words; nor will it do to say that his answer neither had nor didn't have words. Chao Chou left behind all the permutations of logic. Why? If one discusses this matter, it is like sparks struck from stone, like flashing lightning. Only if you set your eyes on it quickly can you see it. If you hesitate and vascillate you won't avoid losing your body and life.

VERSE

Water poured on cannot wet,
> What are you saying? Too deep and far off. What is there to discuss?

Wind blowing cannot enter.
> It's like empty space. Hard, impervious. Address your plea to the sky.

The tiger prowls, the dragon walks;
> He gains independence; he's outstanding.

Ghosts howl, spirits wail.
> Everyone cover your ears! When the wind moves, the grasses bow. Are you not a fellow-student of theirs, Reverend?

His head is three feet long—I wonder who it is!
> A strange being. A sage from where? Do you see? Do you see?

Standing on one foot, he answers back without speaking.
> Bah! He draws back his head and lets his move go. Mountain ghost? He shouldn't be let go, so I strike.

COMMENTARY

"Water poured on cannot wet, wind blowing cannot enter. The tiger prowls, the dragon walks; ghosts howl, spirits wail." There's no place for you to chew on. These four lines versify Chao Chou's answer, which is indeed like a dragon galloping, like a tiger charging. This monk just got an embarrassing situation. Not only this monk; even the ghosts howl, even the spirits wail. It's like when the wind moves, the grasses bow down.

Of the final two lines, it could be said, "One son has intimately understood." "His head is three feet long—I wonder who it is? Standing on one foot, he answers back without speaking." Haven't you heard how a monk asked an Ancient Worthy, "What is the Buddha?" The Ancient Worthy said, "His head is three feet long, his neck two inches long." Hsueh Tou draws on this to use in the verse. I wonder, do you people recognize him? Not even I know him. All at once Hsueh Tou has fully depicted Chao Chou. The real one has always been within: all of you must investigate carefully and try to see it.

Yun Men's Staff Changes into a Dragon

POINTER

Buddhas and sentient beings—fundamentally there is no difference between them. Mountains and rivers and one's own self—how could there be any distinction? Why then is it all divided into two sides?

Even if you can set words turning and occupy the essential bridge, it still won't do to let go. If you don't let go, the whole great earth isn't worth grasping. But what is the place to set words turning? To test, I cite this: look!

CASE

Yun Men showed his staff to the assembly and said,[1] "The staff has changed into a dragon[2] and swallowed the universe.[3] Mountains, rivers, the great earth—where are they to be found?"[4]

NOTES

1. He exposes or transforms according to the occasion. The single-edged sword that kills people, the double-edged sword that brings people to life. He's snatched your eyeballs away.
2. What's the use of so much talk? What's the use of changing?
3. The world's patchrobed monks cannot preserve their lives. Did he block off your throats? Reverend, where will you go to settle your body and establish your life?
4. In the ten directions there are no walls, on the four sides there are no gates. East, west, south, north, the four intermediate points, above, below. How will you handle this one?

COMMENTARY

As for Yun Men's saying, "The staff has changed into a dragon and swallowed the universe. Where are the mountains, rivers, and earth to be found?" If you say it exists, then you are blind; if you say it doesn't exist, then you are dead. Do you see where Yun Men helped people? Bring the staff back to me!

People these days do not understand where Yun Men stood alone and revealed. Instead they say that he went to form to explain mind, that he relied on things to reveal principle. But old Shakyamuni couldn't have not known this theory as he taught the Dharma for forty-nine years; why then did he also need to hold up the flower for Kashyapa's smile? This old fellow caused confusion saying, "I have the treasury of the eye of the correct teaching, the wondrous mind of nirvana—these I pass on to MahaKashyapa." Why was there still a need for the specially transmitted mind seal? Given that all of you are guests in the house of the ancestral teachers, do you understand this specially transmitted mind?

If there is a single thing in your breast, then mountains, rivers, and the great earth appear in profusion before you; if there isn't a single thing in your breast, then outside there is not so much as a fine hair. How can you talk about principle and knowledge fusing, about objective world and mind merging? What's the reason? When one is understood, all are understood; when one is clear, all are clear.

Ch'ang Sha said, "People studying the Path don't know the real, because they've always given recognition to their cognizing mind; this, the basis of countless aeons of births and deaths, fools call the original person." If you suddenly smash the shadowy world of the heaps and elements of life so that body and mind are one likeness and there is nothing else outside your body, you still haven't attained the other half. How can you talk about going to form to reveal the mind, using things to demonstrate principle?

An Ancient said, "As soon as one atom of dust arises, the whole world is contained therein." But say, which atom of dust is this? If you can know this atom of dust, then you can know the staff. As soon as Yun Men picks up his staff, we immediately see his unconfined marvelous activity. Such talk is already a mass of entangling vines, complications; how much the more so is transforming the staff into a dragon! Librarian Ch'ing said, "Has there ever been such talk in the five thousand and forty-eight volumes of the canon?" Every time he turned to his staff, Yun Men brought out the great function of his whole capacity and helped people in a way that was leaping with life.

Pa Chiao said, "If you have a staff, I'll give you a staff; if you have no staff, I'll take your staff away."

Yung Chia said, "This is not an empty exhibition displaying form; it is the actual traces of the Tathagata's precious staff."

Long ago in the time of Dipamkara Buddha, the (future) Tathagata (Shakyamuni) spread his hair to cover some mud for that Buddha. Dipamkara said, "A temple should be built here." Also present then was an elder who thereupon set up a blade of grass right there and said, "The temple has been built." All of you tell me, where is this scene to be found?

The ancestral teacher Hsueh Tou said, "At a blow, experience it; at a shout, receive it rightly." But tell me, receive what rightly? Supposing there's someone who asks, "What is the staff?" Shouldn't you turn a backflip? Shouldn't you clap your hands? All of this would be giving play to your spirits, and has nothing to do with it.

VERSE

The staff swallows the universe—
    What is he saying? The staff is only used for beating dogs.

He vainly talks of peach blossoms floating on the rushing waves.
    Make an opening upwards and all the thousand sages will stand downwind. It's not a matter of grasping clouds and seizing fog. Being able to say it a thousand or ten thousand times isn't as good as catching it in your hand once.

For those with tails burnt off, it's not a matter of grasping clouds and seizing fog;
    I just look to the right and to the left of this. It's just a stick of dry firewood.

Why should the exhausted ones necessarily lose their courage
     and spirit?
          Everyone's temper is like a king's. It's just that you are far
          far away. What will you do about being scared?

I have picked it up—
          Thanks for being so compassionate; you're kindhearted as
          an old lady.

Do you hear or not?
          You can't avoid falling into the weeds. Why hear?

One simply must be completely free and at ease—
          Part-eaten soup, spoiled food. Where does the universe
          come from?

Stop any further mixed up confusion.
          One who quotes this rule has already broken it. It's al-
          ready on your head. I strike and say, "It won't do to let
          go."

With seventy-two blows I'm still letting you off easy—
          I've never carried out this imperative, but if you are going
          to act according to the imperative, it's lucky you found
          me.

Even with one hundred and fifty it's hard to forgive you.
          A just order must be carried out. How could it only be this
          many? Even if he gave three thousand blows in the morn-
          ing and eight hundred blows in the evening, what good
          would it do?

Master Hsueh Tou suddenly picked up his staff and came
     down from his seat; all at once the great assembly
     scattered and fled.
          Why does Hsueh Tou have a dragon's head but a snake's
          tail?

COMMENTARY

Yun Men helps people by a circuitous path; Hsueh Tou helps
people by a direct shortcut. That's why Hsueh Tou discards the
transformation into a dragon; he doesn't need such talk, just
"the staff swallows the universe." Hsueh Tou's great intent is
to have people avoid fanciful interpretations. He goes on to say,

"He vainly talks of peach blossoms floating on the rushing waves." There's no further need for transformations into dragons. At the Gate of Yu there's a three-level rapids; every year by the third month when the peach blossoms bloom and the waves rise, those fish who can go against the current and leap past the rapids change into dragons. Hsueh Tou says even though they change into dragons, this too is still vain talk.

"For those with tails burnt off it's not a matter of grasping clouds and seizing fog." When fish pass through the Gate of Yu a celestial fire burns their tails; they grab the clouds, seize the fog, and depart. Hsueh Tou means that though they change into dragons, it still isn't a matter of grabbing clouds and seizing fog. "Why should the exhausted ones necessarily lose their courage and spirit?" The introduction to Ch'ing Liang's commentary on the Avatamsaka scripture says, "Even bodhisattvas who have accumulated virtuous conduct gasp for breath at the Gate of Yu." His overall meaning is to explain that the realm of the Avatamsaka Flower Garland Cosmos[a] is not something mastered by small virtue or small knowledge; it's like the fish trying to pass through the Dragon Gate of Yu, where those who cannot pass through fail and fall back. They lie in the sand shoals of the dead water, exhausted and gasping. Hsueh Tou means that once they fail and fall back, they always lose their courage and spirit.

"I have picked it up—do you hear or not?" Again he adds footnotes; all at once he's swept it clean for you. All of you "simply must be completely free and at ease—stop any further mixed up confusion." If you go on with mixed up confusion, you have lost the staff.

"With seventy-two blows I'm still letting you off easy—even with a hundred and fifty it's hard to forgive you." Why has Hsueh Tou discarded the heavy for the light? An Ancient said, "Seventy-two blows doubled makes one hundred and fifty." These days people misunderstand and just calculate numerically and say, "It should be seventy-five blows; why is it instead just seventy-two blows?" How far they are from knowing that the Ancient's meaning was beyond the words. Thus it is said, "This matter is not in words and phrases." Hsueh Tou drew on this to use in order to avoid people later on trying to rationalize. Even if you're truly free and at ease, you still rightly deserve to be given seventy-two blows—this is still letting you off easy. Even if you're not free and at ease like this at all, it would be hard to let you go with one hundred and fifty.

Hsueh Tou had completed his verse all at once, yet he picked up his staff again to help some more. Nevertheless, there wasn't even one with blood under his skin.

TRANSLATORS' NOTES

a. The Avatamsaka (Hua-Yen, Kegon) scripture is a major Greater Vehicle Buddhist scripture. The name, which means flower garland or ornament, refers to myriad religious practices, likened to flowers, adorning the realm which is produced as a result of practices in the causal state. It also refers to the representation of myriad qualities and states of being 'adorning' the worlds and universes of the cosmos. In this cosmos, all realms contain infinite realms, ad infinitum, all mutually reflecting and dependent on each other and a moment of thought. Many Ch'an masters were familiar with the Avatamsaka scripture; Tsung-mi, a successor of the Ho-tse line of Southern Ch'an, was also considered the Fifth Patriarch of the Hua-Yen school of Buddhism in China.

Feng Hsueh's One Atom of Dust

POINTER

To set up the Banner of the Teaching and establish its fundamental message is a matter for a genuine master of the school. To judge dragons and snakes, distinguish the initiate from the naive, one must be an accomplished teacher. As for discussing killing and giving life on the edge of a sword, discerning what is appropriate for the moment with a staff, this I leave aside for the moment; just tell me in one phrase how you will assess the matter of occupying the heartland singlehandedly. To test, I cite this:

CASE

Feng Hsueh, giving a talk, said,[1] "If you set up a single atom of dust,[2] the nation flourishes;[3] if you do not set up a single atom of dust,[4] the nation perishes."[5]

Hsueh Tou raised his staff and said,[6] "Are there any patch-robed monks who will live together and die together?"[7]

NOTES

1. He rouses clouds and brings rain. He wants to be host and be guest.
2. "I am king of all things and the autonomous master of all things." Clusters of flowers, clusters of brocade.[a]
3. This is not the business of his house.
4. He sweeps away the tracks and obliterates the traces; having lost his eyes, his nostrils are gone too.
5. Everywhere light shines. What is the use of the nation? This is entirely the business of his house.
6. One must stand like a mile-high wall to accomplish this. Bodhidharma has come.

7. Return the words to me. Although they are right, he wants to even out what is not even. It is necessary to deal with Hsueh Tou to accomplish it. But do you know? If you know, I admit that you are autonomous and free. If you do not know, you get hit three thousand times in the morning, eight hundred times in the evening.

COMMENTARY

As Feng Hsueh said to his assembly, "If you set up a single atom of dust, the nation flourishes; if you don't set up a single atom of dust, the nation perishes." Now tell me, is it right to set up an atom of dust, or is it right not to set up an atom of dust? When you get here, your great function must become manifest before you'll understand. That is why (Feng Hsueh) said, "Even if you can grasp it before it is spoken of, still this is remaining in the shell, wandering in limitation; even if you thoroughly penetrate it at a single phrase, you still won't avoid insane views on the way."

He was a venerable adept in the lineage of Lin Chi; he directly used his own provisions; "If you set up a single atom of dust, the nation flourishes, and the old peasants frown." The meaning lies in the fact that to establish a nation and stabilize the country, it is necessary to rely on crafty ministers and valiant generals; after that, the Unicorn appears, the Pheonix soars—these are the auspicious signs of great peace. How could the people of three-family villages know there are such things? When you do not set up a single atom of dust, the nation perishes, the wind blows chill; why do the old peasants come out and sing hallelujah? Just because the nation has perished. In the (Ts'ao-) Tung lineage, they call this the point of transformation: there is no more Buddha, nor sentient beings; no affirmation, no negation, no good, no bad—it is beyond sound and echo, track or trace. That is why it is said, "Although gold dust is precious, in the eye it obstructs vision."[b] And it is said, "Gold dust is a cataract on the eye; the jewel in one's robe is the defilement of the Dharma.[c] Even one's own spirit is not important; who are the Buddhas and Patriarchs?" Piercing and penetrating supernatural powers and their wondrous action would not be considered exceptional; when he gets here, with his patched robe covering his head, myriad concerns cease—at this time, the mountain monk does not understand anything at all. If one were to speak any more of mind, speak of nature, speak of the profound, speak of the wondrous, it would not be any use at all. What is the reason? "He has his own mountain spirit realm."

Nan Ch'uan said to his community, "The seven hundred eminent monks on Huang Mei were all men who understood the Buddha Dharma. They did not get his Robe and Bowl; there was only workman Lu who did not understand the Buddha Dharma—that is why he got his robe and bowl."[d]

He also said, "The Buddhas of the past, present, and future do not know what is; but cats and oxen do know what is." The old peasants either frown or sing, but tell me how you will understand? And tell me, what eye do they possess, that they are like this? You should know that in front of the old peasants' gates no ordinances are posted.

Hsueh Tou, having raised both sides, finally lifts up his staff and says, "Are there any patchrobed monks who will live together and die together?" At that time, if there had been a fellow who could come forth and utter a phrase, alternately acting as guest and host, he would have avoided this old fellow Hsueh Tou's pointing to himself in the end.

VERSE

The old peasants may not unfurrow their brows,
> There is someone three thousand miles away. Delicious food is not for a satisfied man to eat.

But for now I hope that the nation establishes a sturdy foundation.
> The one song of great peace, everyone knows. When you want to go, go; when you want to stay, stay. Heaven, earth, the whole world is one gate of liberation. How will you establish it?

Crafty ministers, valiant generals—where are they now?
> Are there any? Are there? The land is broad, the people are few, and rarely is anyone met with. But do not point to yourself.

Ten thousand miles' pure wind, only I know.
If there is no one by your side, who will you have sweep
the ground? Here's another cloud-dwelling saint.

COMMENTARY

Previously he quoted both sides; here, instead, he just raises
one side and lets the other go. He cuts down the long and adds
to the short, abandons the heavy and goes along with the light.
That is why he says, "The old peasants may not unfurrow their
brows, but for now I hope the nation establishes a sturdy foundation; where are the crafty ministers and valiant generals
now?" When Hsueh Tou lifted up his staff and said, "Are there
any patchrobed monks who will live together and die together?" This was just like saying, "Are there still any crafty
ministers and valiant generals?" In one gulp he has swallowed
everyone completely. That is why I say that the land is broad,
the people few, and rarely is anyone met with. Are there any
who know? Come forth and be buried in the same pit. "Ten
thousand miles' pure wind, only I know." This is where Hsueh
Tou points to himself.

TRANSLATORS' NOTES

a.   Clusters of flowers and brocade refer to spring and autumn, which
     in turn symbolize birth and death.
b.   Gold dust in the eyes symbolizes attachment to the Buddha
     Dharma, the teaching of enlightenment; the Diamond Cutter
     scripture says that even the Dharma should be abandoned, let
     alone what is not Dharma.
c.   The jewel in one's robe symbolizes Buddha-nature, the potential
     of enlightenment inherent in everyone; the defilement of the
     Dharma means attachment to the Dharma, maintaining a sense
     of attainment; pride, however subtle, in one's faith, practice, or
     accomplishment.
d.   Huang Mei was the mountain abode of Hung Jen, the Fifth Pa-
     triarch of Ch'an in China; workman Lu was an illiterate woodcut-
     ter who came to the community of Hung Jen and was later chosen
     as the latter's successor. After fifteen years travelling anony-

mously with a band of hunters, he "appeared" in south China, with the robe and bowl, signifying the inheritance of the Dharma, of the Fifth Patriarch. He was known as Hui Neng (his name), Ts'ao Ch'i (the name of the place he lived as a teacher), and workman Lu; he was the sixth and perhaps most illustrious patriarch of Ch'an.

Yun Men's Within There Is a Jewel

POINTER

By means of the knowledge that has no teacher, he produces the marvelous function of non-doing; by means of unconditional compassion, he acts unasked as an excellent friend. In one phrase there is killing, there is giving life; in one act there is releasing, there is holding. Tell me, who has ever been like this? To test, I cite this to see.

CASE

Yun Men said to the community, "Within heaven and earth,[1] through space and time,[2] there is a jewel,[3] hidden inside the mountain of form.[4] Pick up a lamp and go into the Buddha-hall;[5] take the triple gate[a] and bring it on the lamp."[6]

NOTES

1. The land is broad, the people few. The six directions cannot contain it.
2. Stop making your living in a ghost cave. You already missed it.
3. Where is it? Light is produced. I only fear that you'll seek it in a ghost cave.
4. A confrontation. Check!
5. It still can be discussed.
6. Great Master Yun Men is right, but nevertheless difficult to understand. He seems to have gotten somewhere. If you examine thoroughly, you will not avoid the smell of shit.

COMMENTARY

Yun Men says, "Within heaven and earth, through space and time, there is a jewel, hidden in the mountain of form." Now tell me, is Yun Men's meaning in the "fishing pole,"[b] or is the meaning in the lamp? These lines are paraphrased from a treatise of Seng Chao, Master of the Teachings, called *Jewel Treasury*; Yun Men brought them up to teach his community.

In the time of the Latter Ch'in, Seng Chao was in the Garden of Freedom composing his treatise. When he was copying the old *Vimalakirtinirdesa* scripture he realized that Chuang-tzu and Lao-tzu had still not exhausted the marvel; Chao then paid obeisance to Kumarajiva as his teacher. He also called on the bodhisattva Buddhabhadra at the Tile Coffin Temple, who had transmitted the Mind Seal from the Twenty-seventh Patriarch (Prajnatara) in India. Chao entered deeply into the inner sanctum. One day Chao ran into trouble; when he was about to be executed, he asked for seven days' reprieve, during which time he composed the treatise *Jewel Treasury*.

So Yun Men cited four phrases from that treatise to teach his community. The main idea is "how can you take a priceless jewel and conceal it in the heaps and elements?" The words spoken in the treatise are all in accord with the talk of our school. Have you not seen how Ching Ch'ing asked Ts'ao Shan, "How is it when in the principle of pure emptiness ultimately there is no body?" Ts'ao Shan said, "The principle being like this, what about phenomena?" Ch'ing said, "As is principle, so are phenomena." Shan said, "You can fool me, one person, but what can you do about the eyes of all the sages?" Ch'ing said, "Without the eyes of all the sages, how could you know it is not so?" Shan said, "Officially, not even a needle is admitted; privately, even a cart and horse can pass."

That is why it was said, "Within heaven and earth, in space and time, there is a jewel, hidden in the mountain of form." The great meaning of this is to show that everyone is fully endowed, each individual is perfectly complete. Yun Men thus brought it up to show his community; it is totally obvious—he couldn't go on and add interpretations for you like a lecturer. But he is compassionate and adds a footnote for you, saying, "Pick up a lamp and go into the Buddha-hall; bring the triple gate on the lamp."

Now tell me, when Yun Men speaks this way, what is his meaning? Have you not seen how an Ancient said, "The true nature of ignorance is identical to Buddhahood; the empty body of illusion is identical to the body of reality." It is also said, "See the Buddha mind right in the ordinary mind."

The "mountain of form" is the four gross elements and five heaps (which constitute human life).ᶜ "Within there is a jewel, hidden in the mountain of form." That is why it is said, "All Buddhas are in the mind; deluded people go seeking outside. Though within they embosom a priceless jewel, they do not know it, and let it rest there all their lives." It is also said, "The Buddha-nature clearly manifests, but the sentient beings dwelling in form hardly see it. If one realizes that sentient beings have no self, how does his own face differ from a Buddha's face?" "The mind is the original mind; the face is the face born of woman—the Rock of Ages may be moved, but here there is no change."

Some people acknowledge this radiant shining spirituality as the jewel; but they cannot make use of it, and they do not realize its wondrousness. Therefore they cannot set it in motion and cannot bring it out in action. An Ancient said, "Reaching an impasse, then change; having changed, then you can pass through."

"Pick up a lamp and head into the Buddha-hall"; if it is a matter of ordinary sense, this can be fathomed—but can you fathom "bring the triple gate on the lamp"? Yun Men has broken up emotional discrimination, intellectual ideas, gain, loss, affirmation, and negation, all at once for you. Hsueh Tou has said, "I like the freshly established devices of Shao Yang (Yun Men); all his life he pulled out nails and drew out pegs for others." He also said, "I do not know how many sit on the chair of rank; but the sharp sword cutting away causes others' admiration." When he said, "Pick up a lamp and go into the Buddha-hall," this one phrase has already cut off completely; yet, "bring the triple gate on the lamp." If you discuss this matter, it is like sparks struck from stone, like the flash of a lightning bolt. Yun Men said, "If you would attain, just seek a way of entry; Buddhas numerous as atoms are under your feet, the three treasuries of the holy teachings are on your tongues; (but) this is not as good as being enlightened. Monks, do not think falsely; sky is sky, earth is earth, mountains are mountains, rivers are rivers, monks are monks, lay people are lay people." After a long pause he said, "Bring me the immovable mountain before you." Then a monk came forth and asked, "How is it when a student sees that mountains are mountains and rivers are rivers?" Yun Men drew a line with his hand and

said, "Why is the triple gate going from here?" He feared you
would die, so he said, "When you know, it is the superb flavor
of ghee; if you do not know, instead it becomes poison."

This is why it is said, "When completely thoroughly understood, there is nothing to understand; the most abstruse profundity of the mystery is still to be scorned."

Hsueh Tou again brought it up and said, "Within heaven and
earth, through space and time, therein is a jewel; it lies hidden
in the mountain of form. It is hung on a wall; for nine years
Bodhidharma did not dare to look at it straight on. If any patchrobed monk wants to see it now, I will hit him right on the
spine with my staff."[d] See how these self-possessed teachers of
our school never use any actual doctrine to tie people up.
Hsuan Sha said, "Though you try to enmesh him in a trap, he
doesn't consent to stay; though you call after him, he doesn't
turn his head. Even though he is like this, still he is a sacred
tortoise dragging his tail."

VERSE

Look! Look!
　　Set your eyes on high. Why look? A black dragon admires
　　a gem.

On the ancient embankment, who holds the fishing pole?
　　Alone, quite alone; stolid, quite stolid. Hsueh Tou draws
　　his bow after the thief has gone. If you see jowls on the
　　back of someone's head, don't have anything to do with
　　him.

Clouds roll on.
　　Cut them off. A hundred layers, a thousand levels. A
　　greasy hat and stinking shirt.

The water, vast and boundless—
　　Left and right it goes, blocking in front and supporting in
　　back.

The white flowers in the moonlight, you must see for yourself.
　　When you see them, you'll go blind. If you can com-
　　prehend Yun Men's words, then you will see Hsueh Tou's
　　last phrase.

COMMENTARY

If you can comprehend Yun Men's words, then you will see how Hsueh Tou helps people. He goes to the last two phrases of Yun Men's address to the community and there gives you a footnote saying, "Look! Look!" If you thereupon make raising your eyebrows and glinting your eyes your understanding,[e] you are out of touch.

An Ancient said, "The spiritual light shines alone, far transcending the senses; the essential substance is manifest, real and eternal. It is not captured in written letters. The nature of mind has no defilement; it is basically naturally perfectly complete. Just get rid of delusive clingings and merge with the Buddha that is as is." If you just go to raising your eyebrows and glinting your eyes and sit there forever, how will you be able to transcend the senses?

Hsueh Tou is saying, "Look! Look!" Yun Men appears to be on an ancient embankment holding a fishing pole; the clouds are rolling and the water is vast and boundless. The bright moon reflects white flowers, and white flowers reflect the bright moon. At this moment, tell me, what realm is this? If you can perceive it immediately and directly, the former and the latter phrases are just like one phrase.

TRANSLATORS' NOTES

a.   The triple gate is the main gate of a monastery; usually it comprises three gates, hence the name, but it is called the triple gate even if there is only one. It is also called the "mountain gate," since monasteries were referred to as "mountains" even if they were not actually so situated. Many Ch'an monasteries, especially in the earlier days, were actually in the mountains, hence the name.

b.   See Hsueh Tou's verse; Yun Men's saying is likened to a "fishing pole." The idea of "fishing" as one of the strategies of a teaching Ch'an master has been met with several times in this book.

c.   The four gross elements are earth, air, fire, and water; the five heaps are form, sensation, perception, synergies, and consciousness. These classifications represent the elements of existence in general, of human life in particular. The analysis of the human being into five 'heaps' is to show that there is no real self or soul, no individual self-subsistent entity.

d.   This is from the *Hsueh Tou Hou Lu*, "Later Record of Hsueh Tou".

e.   Tenkei says this means making a show of meditational effort.

Nan Ch'uan Kills a Cat

POINTER

Where the road of ideation cannot reach, that is just right to bring to attention; where verbal explanation cannot reach, you must set your eyes on it quickly. If your thunder rolls and comets fly, then you can overturn lakes and topple mountains. Is there anyone in the crowd who can manage this? To test, I cite this to see.

CASE

At Nan Ch'uan's place one day the (monks of) the eastern and western halls were arguing about a cat.[1] When Nan Ch'uan saw this, he then held up the cat and said, "If you can speak, then I will not kill it."[2] No one in the community replied;[3] Nan Ch'uan cut the cat into two pieces.[4]

NOTES

1. It's not just today that they're haggling together. This is a case of degeneracy.
2. When the true imperative goes into effect, the ten directions are subdued. This old fellow has the capability to distinguish dragons from snakes.
3. What a pity to let him go. A bunch of lacquer tubs—what are they worth? Phoney Ch'an followers are as plentiful as hemp and millet.
4. How quick! How quick! If he hadn't acted like this, they would all be fellows playing with a mud ball. He draws the bow after the thief has gone. Already this is secondary; he should have been hit before he even picked it up.

COMMENTARY

An accomplished master of our school: see his movement, stillness, his going out and entering in. Tell me, what was his inner meaning? This story about killing the cat is widely discussed in monasteries everywhere. Some say that the holding up is it; some say it lies in the cutting. But actually these bear no relation to it at all. If he had not held it up, then would you still spin out all sorts of rationalizations? You are far from knowing that this Ancient had the eye to judge heaven and earth, and he had the sword to settle heaven and earth.

Now you tell me, after all, who was it that killed the cat? Just when Nan Ch'uan held it up and said, "If you can speak, then I won't kill it," at that moment, if there were suddenly someone who could speak, tell me, would Nan Ch'uan have killed it or not? This is why I say, "When the true imperative goes into effect, the ten directions are subdued." Stick your head out beyond the heavens and look; who's there?

The fact is that at that time he really did not kill. This story does not lie in killing or not killing. This matter is clearly known; it is so distinctly clear. It is not to be found in emotions or opinions; if you go searching in emotions and opinions, then you turn against Nan Ch'uan. Just see it right on the edge of the knife. If it exists, all right; if it does not exist, all right; if it neither exists nor doesn't exist, that is all right too. That is why an Ancient said, "When at an impasse, change; when you change, then you can pass through." People nowadays do not know how to change and pass through; they only go running to the spoken words. When Nan Ch'uan held up (the cat) in this way, he could not have been telling people they should be able to say something; he just wanted people to attain on their own, each act on their own, and know for themselves. If you do not understand it in this way, after all you will grope without finding it. Hsueh Tou versifies it directly:

VERSE

In both halls they are phoney Ch'an followers:
   Familiar words come from a familiar mouth. With one
   phrase he has said it all. He settles the case according to
   the facts.

Stirring up smoke and dust, they are helpless.
>Look; what settlement will you make? A completely ob-
>vious public case. Still there's something here.

Fortunately, there is Nan Ch'uan, who is able to uphold the
command:
>Raising my whisk, I say, "It's just like this." Old Master
>Wang (Nan Ch'uan) amounts to something. He uses the
>fine jewel-sword of the Diamond King to cut mud.

With one stroke of the knife he cuts into two pieces, letting
them be lopsided as they may.
>Shattered into a hundred fragments. If someone should
>suddenly hold his knife still, see what he would do. He
>can't be let go, so I strike!

COMMENTARY

"In both halls they are phoney Ch'an followers." Hsueh Tou
does not die at the phrase, and he also does not acknowledge
that which is ahead of a donkey but behind a horse. He has a
place to turn, so he says, "Stirring up smoke and dust, they are
helpless." Hsueh Tou and Nan Ch'uan walk hand in hand; in
one phrase he has said it all. The leaders of the two halls have
no place to rest their heads; everywhere they go, they just stir
up smoke and dust, unable to accomplish anything. Fortunately there is Nan Ch'uan to settle this public case for them,
and he wraps it up cleanly and thoroughly. But what can be
done for them, who neither reached home nor got to the shop?
That is why he said, "Fortunately there is Nan Ch'uan, who is
able to uphold the command; with one stroke of the knife he
cuts into two pieces, letting them be lopsided as they may." He
directly cuts in two with one knife, without further concern as
to whether they'll be unevenly lopsided. But tell me, what
command is Nan Ch'uan enforcing?

Nan Ch'uan Questions Chao Chou

CASE

Nan Ch'uan recited the preceding story to question Chao Chou.[1] Chou immediately took off his straw sandals, placed them on his head, and left.[2] Nan Ch'uan said, "If you had been here, you could have saved the cat."[3]

NOTES

1. They must be of like hearts and like minds before this is possible. Only one on the same road would know.
2. He does not avoid trailing mud and dripping water.
3. Singing and clapping, they accompany each other; those who know the tune are few. He adds error to error.

COMMENTARY

Chao Chou was Nan Ch'uan's true heir; when Nan Ch'uan spoke of the head, Chao Chou understood the tail; when it is brought up, he immediately knows where it comes down.

In the evening Nan Ch'uan repeated the preceding story and asked Chao Chou about it. Chou was an old adept; he immediately took off his straw sandals, put them on his head, and left. Ch'uan said, "If you had been here, you could have saved the cat." But tell me, was it really like this or not? Nan Ch'uan said, "If you can speak, then I won't kill it." Like a flint-struck spark, like a flash of lightning. Chao Chou immediately took off his sandals, put them on his head, and left; he studied the living word, not the dead word—each day renewed, each moment renewed; even the thousand sages could not stir a hairsbreadth. You must bring forth your own family treasure; only then will you see the great function of his total capacity. He is saying, "I am King of Dharma, free in all respects."[a]

Many people misunderstand and say that Chao Chou temporarily made his sandals into the cat. Some say he meant, "When you say, 'If you can speak, then I won't kill it,' I would then put my sandals on my head and leave. It's just you killing the cat—it is none of my business." But this has nothing to do with it; this is just giving play to the spirit. You are far from knowing that the Ancient's meaning was like the universal cover of the sky, like the universal support of the earth.

That father and son conformed with each other; the edges of their activity met with each other. When Nan Ch'uan raised the head, Chao Chou immediately understood the tail. Students these days do not know the turning point of the Ancients, and vainly go to the road of ideation to figure them out. If you want to see, just go to Nan Ch'uan's and Chao Chou's turning points and you will see them well.

VERSE

The public case completed, he questions Chao Chou:
  The words are still in our ears. No use to cut any more. He hangs a medicine bag on the back of a hearse.

In the city of Ch'ang An, he's free to wander at leisure.[b]
  He has attained such joyful liveliness; he has attained such freedom. He lets his hands pick the plants. I cannot but let you go on this way.

His straw sandals he wears on his head—no one understands;
  Yet there is one or a half. This is a special style. Light is fitting, darkness is also fitting.

Returning to his native village, then he rests.
  You should be given thirty blows right where you stand. But tell me, where is the fault? It's just that you are raising waves where there is no wind. They let each other off. I only fear you will not be thus; if so, it's quite unusual.

COMMENTARY

"The public case completed, he questions Chao Chou." The librarian Ch'ing said, "It is like a man settling a case; eight strokes of the staff is eight strokes; thirteen is thirteen. Already he has settled it completely. Yet he then brings it up to ask Chao Chou."

Chao Chou was a man of his household and understood the essence of Nan Ch'uan's meaning. He was a man who had thoroughly passed through; struck, he resounds and immediately rolls. He possesses the eyes and brain of a genuine adept; as soon as he hears it mentioned, he immediately gets up and acts.

Hsueh Tou says, "In the city of Ch'ang An, he is free to roam at leisure." He is quite a dotard. An Ancient said, "Although Ch'ang An is pleasant, it is not a place to stay for long." It has also been said, "Ch'ang An is quite noisy; my province is peaceful." Still, you must recognize what is appropriate to the situation and distinguish good and bad before you will understand.

"His grass sandals he wears on his head—no one understands." When he put the sandals on his head, this bit, though without so much ado, is why it is said, "Only I myself can know, only I myself can experience it." Then you will be able to see how Nan Ch'uan, Chao Chou, and Hsueh Tou attained alike and acted alike.

But tell me, right now, how will you understand? "Returning to his native village, then he rests." What place is his native village? If he didn't understand, he surely wouldn't speak this way. Since he did understand, tell me, where is the native village. I strike immediately.

TRANSLATORS' NOTES

a. This phrase is taken from the *Saddharmapundarika* scripture, where it refers to the Buddha's independent mastery in the use of teachings, provisional or true, in a manner appropriate to the time, situation, and capacities of the hearers.

b. Commentaries explain variously that this second line refers to Nan Ch'uan, to Chao Chou, or to both. Ch'ang An, which name means "eternal peace," was at various times a capital of the Chinese empire. As "the capital," it was used in Ch'an to refer to enlightenment; that one should not dwell forever in Ch'ang An is a re-statement of the admonition to transcend all sense of attainment, not to be attached to the Dharma.

An Outsider Questions the Buddha

POINTER

Appearing without form, filling the ten directions of space, expanding everywhere equally; responding without mind, extending over lands and seas without trouble; understanding three when one is raised, judging grains and ounces at the glance of an eye. Even if the blows of your staff fall like rain and your shouts are like thunder rolling, still you have not yet filled the footsteps of a trancendent man. But tell me, what is the business of a transcendent man? Try to see.

CASE

An outsider asked the Buddha, "I do not ask about the spoken or the unspoken."[1] The World Honored One remained silent.[2] The outsider sighed in admiration and said, "The World Honored One's great kindness and great compassion have opened up my clouds of illusion and let me gain entry."[3]

After the outsider had left, Ananda asked the Buddha, "What did the outsider realize, that he said he had gained entry?"[4] The Buddha said, "Like a good horse, he goes as soon as he sees the shadow of the whip."[5]

NOTES

1. Although he is not a member of the household, still he has a bit of a fragrant air. Twin swords fly through space. It's lucky he doesn't ask.
2. Do not slander the World Honored One; his voice is like thunder. No one sitting or standing here could move him.
3. A sharp fellow—one push and he rolls, a bright pearl in a bowl.
4. He can't avoid making others doubt; still he wants everyone to know. He is trying to repair a pot with cold iron.

5. Tell me, what do you call the shadow of the whip? Striking with my whisk, (I say) on the staff there is an eye bright as the sun. If you want to know if it is real gold, see it through fire. Having gotten a mouth, eat.

COMMENTARY

If this matter were in words and phrases, do not the twelve parts of the Teachings of the Three Vehicles contain words and phrases? Some say it is right just not to speak. Then what would have been the use of the Patriarch's coming from the West? As for so many public cases which have come down from ancient times, after all how will you see what they are getting at?

This one public case is understood verbally by quite a few people. Some call it remaining silent, some call it remaining seated, and some call it silently not answering. But fortunately none of this has anything to do with it; how could you ever manage to find it by groping around? This matter really isn't in words and phrases, yet it is not apart from words and phrases. If you have the slightest bit of hesitation, then you are a thousand miles, ten thousand miles away. See how after that outsider had intuitively awakened, only then did he realize that it is neither here nor there, neither in affirmation nor in negation. But tell me, what is this?

Master I Huai of T'ien I made a verse which said,

> Vimalakirti was not silent, did not remain that
> way;[a]
> Sitting on his seat engaged in deliberation, he made
> an error.
> Though the sharp sword is in its scabbard, its chill
> light is cold;
> Outsiders and celestial demons all fold their hands
> helplessly.

When Master Tao Ch'ang of Pai Chang was studying with Fa Yen, Yen had him contemplate this story. Fa Yen one day asked him, "What incident are you contemplating?" Ch'ang said, "The outsider questioning the Buddha." Yen said, "Stop! Stop! You're about to go to his silence to understand, aren't you?" At these words Ch'ang was suddenly greatly enlightened. Later, in teaching his community, he said, "On Pai Chang there are three secrets; 'drink tea,' 'take care,' and 'rest.' If you still try to think any more about them, I know you are still not through."

"Breast-beater Chen" of Ts'ui Yen cited (this case) and said, "In the six directions and nine states, blue, yellow, red, and white each intermingle."

The outsider knew the four Vedas and told himself he was omniscient; everywhere he was, he drew people into discussions. He posed a question, hoping to cut off old Shakya Buddha's tongue. The World Honored One did not expend any energy, yet the outsider was immediately awakened. He sighed in admiration and said, "The World Honored One's great kindness and great compassion have opened up the clouds of my confusion and allowed me to gain entry."

But tell me, where are the World Honored One's great kindness and compassion? The World Honored One's single eye sees through past, present, and future; the outsider's twin pupils penetrate the Indian continent.

Chen Ju of Kuei Shan brought this up and said,

> The heretic had the most precious jewel hidden
>   within;
> The World Honored One kindly lifted it on high for
>   him.
> Forests of patterns are clearly revealed,
> Myriad forms are evident.

But after all, what did the outsider realize? It was like chasing a dog towards a fence: when he gets as far as is possible, when there is no way to get by, he must turn around and come back; then he will be leaping lively. If you cast away judgement and comparison and affirmation and negation all at once, your emotions ended and your views gone, it will naturally become thoroughly obvious.

After the outsider had left, Ananda asked the Buddha, "What did the outsider realize, that he said he had gained entry?" The Buddha said, "Like a good horse, he goes as soon as he sees the shadow of the whip." Since then, everywhere it has been said that at this point even he was blown by the wind into a different tune. It has also been said that he had a dragon's head but a snake's tail. Where is the shadow of the World Honored One's whip? Where is the seeing of the shadow of the whip? Hsueh Tou said, "False and true are not separate; the fault comes from the shadow of the whip."

Chen Ju said, "Ananda's golden bell is rung twice, and everyone hears it together. Even though this is so, it is very much like two dragons fighting for a jewel. It matured the majestic dragon of that other wise one."

VERSE

The wheel of potential has never turned;
　　It is here. After all it doesn't move a bit.

If it turns, it will surely go two ways.
　　If it doesn't fall into existence, it will surely fall into
　　nonexistence; if it doesn't go east, then it will go west.
　　The left eye is half a pound, the right eye eight ounces.

A clear mirror is suddenly leaned on a stand,
　　But do you see old Shakyamuni? One push and it turns.
　　Broken! Broken! Scattered! Scattered!

And immediately distinguishes beautiful and ugly.
　　The whole world is the gate of liberation. I should give
　　you thirty blows of the staff. But do you see old
　　Shakyamuni?

Beautiful and ugly distinct, the clouds of illusion open.
　　He lets out a pathway. I allow as you have a place to turn
　　your body, but nevertheless you're just an outsider.

In the gate of compassion, where is any dust produced?
　　The whole world has never concealed it. Retreat;
　　retreat—Bodhidharma has come.

Thus I think of a good horse seeing the whip's shadow:
　　I have a staff; there's no need for you to give me one. But
　　tell me, where is the shadow of the whip, and where is the
　　good horse?

Gone a thousand miles in pursuit of the wind, I call him back;
　　Riding on the Buddha-hall, I go out the main gate. If he
　　turns around, he goes wrong. He shouldn't be let go, so I
　　strike.

Calling, if I get him to return, I'd snap my fingers thrice.
He neither reaches the village nor gets to the shop. With
your staff broken, where will you go? The sound of Hsueh
Tou's thunder is great, but there is no rain at all.

COMMENTARY

"The wheel of potential has never turned; if it turns it will
surely go two ways." The "potential" is the spiritual potential
of the thousand sages; the "wheel" is the original lifeline of all
people. Have you not read Hsueh Tou's saying,

> *The spiritual potential of the thousand sages is not*
> *easily approached;*
> *Dragon's sons born of dragons, do not be irresolute.*
> *Chao Chou has stolen a gem worth many cities;*
> *The King of Ch'in and Hsiang Ju both lose their*
> *lives.*[b]

The outsider, after all, was able to hold it still and be the
master; he never moved at all. How so? He said, "I do not ask
about the spoken or the unspoken." Is this not the entirety of
potential?

The World Honored One knew how to observe the wind to
set the sail, how to give medicine in accordance with the disease; that is why he remained silent. The entire potential up-
lifted, the outsider merged with it completely; his wheel of
potential then turned freely and smoothly: it neither turned
towards existence nor nonexistence; it did not fall into gain or
loss, was not bound by the ordinary or the holy—both sides
were cut off at once. Just as the World Honored One remained
silent, the other bowed. Many people nowadays fall into
nonexistence, or else they fall into existence; they only remain
within being and non-being, running either way.

Hsueh Tou says, "A clear mirror is suddenly leaned on a
stand, and immediately distinguishes beautiful and ugly." This
has never moved; it just calls for silence, like a clear mirror
leaning on its stand—myriad forms cannot avoid their appearance.

The outsider said, "The World Honored One's great kindness and compassion have opened my clouds of illusion and

allowed me to gain entry." Tell me, where is the outsider's point of entry? At this point, you must each seek on your own, investigate on your own, awaken on your own, and understand on your own before you will find it. Then in all places, walking, standing, sitting, and lying, without question of high or low, all at once it is completely manifest and does not move at all anymore. The moment they make judgements and comparisons, or have the slightest hair of rationalization, then this blocks people up completely, and there is no more ability to enter actively.

The last part versifies, "The World Honored One's great kindness and great compassion have opened up the clouds of my illusion and allowed me to gain entry." Right away he abruptly distinguishes beautiful and ugly; "Beautiful and ugly distinct, the clouds of illusion open; in the gate of compassion, where is any dust produced?" The whole world is the door of the World Honored One's great compassion. If you can pass through, it's not worth grasping. This also is an open door. Have you not read how the World Honored One contemplated this matter for twenty-one days—"I would rather not explain the truth, but quickly enter extinction."

"So I think of a good horse seeing the shadow of the whip; gone a thousand miles in pursuit of the wind, I call him back." A "wind-chasing" horse, seeing the shadow of a whip, immediately goes a thousand miles; if you make it return, it returns. Hsueh Tou intends to praise him by saying, "If you find an excellent breed, then you can give one push, and he immediately rolls; one call, and he immediately comes back. Calling, if I get him to return, I'd snap my fingers thrice." But tell me, is this criticism, or is it scattering sand?

TRANSLATORS' NOTES

a. In the scripture spoken by Vimalakirti (*Vimalakirtinirdesasutra*), after hearing a number of bodhisattvas give eloquent explanations of non-duality, the enlightened layman Vimalakirti gave his explanation of non-duality by not saying anything; Manjusri, the embodiment of wisdom, praised this explanation as most eloquent. (See Case 84.)

b. Hsiang Ju was a minister of the King of Chao in the early third
    century B.C., during the "Warring States" period; he was sent to
    offer a rare gem to the king of Ch'in (a neighboring state in what is
    now northern China) in exchange for dominion over fifteen cities.
    After presenting the gem, Hsiang Ju perceived that the king of
    Ch'in was reluctant to keep his part of the bargain; so he used a
    ruse to get the gem back, and had it returned secretly to the
    kingdom of Chao. In this poem from his *Tsu Ying Chi* ("Collec-
    tion on Outstanding Ancestors"), Hsueh Tou constructs a simile
    based on the name of Chao Chou, the place where the great Ch'an
    master Ts'ung Shen (778-897) lived. He was called by the name of
    the place, which had been in the ancient Kingdom of Chao. The
    King of Ch'in and Hsiang Ju represent opposition; the Buddha,
    represented by Ch'an master Chao Chou, cuts off opposition by
    taking away the object of contention.

Yen T'ou's Getting Huang Ch'ao's Sword

POINTER

Meeting the situation head-on, setting a pitfall for a tiger; attacking from front and side, laying out strategy to capture a thief. Adapting in light and adapting in darkness, letting both go or gathering both in, knowing how to play with a deadly snake—all this is a matter for an adept.

CASE

Yen T'ou asked a monk, "Where do you come from?"[1]
The monk said, "From the Western Capital."[2]
Yen T'ou said, "After Huang Ch'ao had gone, did you get his sword?"[3]
The monk said, "I got it."[4]
Yen T'ou extended his neck, came near and said, "Yaa!"[5]
The monk said, "Your head has fallen, Master."[6] Yen T'ou laughed out loud.[7]
Later that monk went to Hsueh Feng.[8] Feng asked, "Where did you come from?"[9] The monk said, "From Yen T'ou."[10] Hsueh Feng said, "What did he have to say?"[11] The monk recounted the preceding story.[12] Hsueh Feng hit him thirty blows with his staff and drove him out.[13]

NOTES

1. He is defeated before he even opens his mouth. (Yen T'ou) is boring into a skullbone. If you want to know where he's coming from, it's not hard.
2. After all, he's a petty thief.
3. Yen T'ou has never been a petty thief. He doesn't fear losing his head, so he asks such a question: he's very courageous indeed!

4. He's defeated, but doesn't know where to turn. Ignoramuses are as plentiful as hemp and millet.

5. He must know what's appropriate to the moment, to do this. This is a pitfall to catch a tiger. What is going on in his mind?

6. He only sees the sharpness of the awl; he does not see the squareness of the chisel. What good or bad does he know? He's struck!

7. No patchrobed monk in the world can do anything to him. He completely fools everyone in the world. No one can find out where this old fellow's head has fallen.

8. As before, he is fatheaded and stupid. This monk is thoroughly defeated time and again.

9. He cannot but tell where he comes from; but still Hsueh Feng wants to try him.

10. After all he is defeated.

11. If he can recite it, he won't avoid getting hit.

12. Right then he should be driven out.

13. Although it is true that he cuts nails and shears through iron, why does he only strike thirty blows with his staff? He hasn't yet gotten to the point where his staff breaks. This is not yet the real thing. Why? "Three thousand blows in the morning, eight hundred blows in the evening." If (Hsueh Feng) were not a fellow student (with Yen T'ou), how could he discern the point? Although this is so, just tell me, where do Hsueh Feng and Yen T'ou abide?

COMMENTARY

Whenever you carry your bag and bowl, pulling out the weeds seeking the Way, you must first possess the foot-travelling eye. This monk's eyes were like comets, yet he was still thoroughly exposed by Yen T'ou, and pierced all the way through on a single string. At that time, if he had been a man, whether it were to kill or to enliven, he would have made use of it immediately as soon as it was brought up. But this monk was a rickety dotard and instead said, "I got it." If you travel on foot like this, the King of Death will question you and demand you pay your grocery bill. I don't know how many straw sandals he wore out until he got to Hsueh Feng. At that time, if he had had a little bit of eye power, then he would have been able to get a glimpse; wouldn't that have felt good?

This story has a knotty complication in it. Although this matter has neither gain nor loss, the gain and loss are tremendous: although there is no picking and choosing, when you get here, you after all must possess the eyes to pick and choose.

See how when Lung Ya was travelling on foot, he posed this question to Te Shan: "How is it when the student wants to take the Master's head with a sharp sword?" Te Shan stretched out his neck, approached, and said, "Yaa!" Lung Ya said, "The Master's head has fallen." Te Shan returned to the abbot's room. Lung Ya later recited this to Tung Shan. Tung Shan said, "What did Te Shan say at the time?" Lung Ya said, "He said nothing." Tung Shan said, "His having nothing to say, I leave aside for the moment: just bring Te Shan's fallen head for me to see." Lung Ya at these words was greatly awakened; later he burned incense, and gazing far off towards Te Shan, he bowed and repented. A monk repeated this to Te Shan. Te Shan said, "Old man Tung Shan does not know good from bad; this fellow has been dead for so long, even if you could revive him, what would be the use?"

This public case is the same as that of Lung Ya: Te Shan returned to the abbot's room; thus in darkness he was most wonderful. Yen T'ou laughs loudly—in his laugh there is poison: if any one could discern it, he could travel freely throughout the world. If this monk had been able to pick it out at that moment, he would have escaped critical examination for all time. But at Yen T'ou's place, he had already missed it. Observe that old man Hsueh Feng; being a fellow student (with Yen T'ou), he immediately knew where he was at. Still, he didn't explain it all for that monk, but just hit him thirty blows of the staff and drove him out of the monastery. Thereby he was "before light and after annihilation." This is the method of holding up the nostrils of an adept patchrobed monk to help the person; he doesn't do anything else for him, but makes him awaken on his own.

When genuine teachers of our school help people, sometimes they trap them and do not let them come out; sometimes they release them and let them be slovenly. After all, they must have a place to appear. Yen T'ou and Hsueh Feng, supposedly so great, were on the contrary exposed by this rice-eating Ch'an follower. When Yen T'ou said, "After Huang Ch'ao had gone, did you get his sword?" People, tell me, what could be said here to avoid his laughter, and to avoid Hsueh Feng's brandishing his staff and driving him out? Here it is difficult to understand; if you have never personally witnessed and personally awakened, even if your mouth is swift and sharp to the very end, you will not be able to pass through and out of birth and death. I always teach people to observe the pivot of this action; if you hesitate, you are far, far away from it. Have you not seen how T'ou Tzu asked a monk from Yen Ping, "Have you brought a sword?" The monk pointed at the ground with his hand. T'ou Tzu said, "For thirty years I have been handling horses, but today I have been kicked by a mule." Look at that monk; he too was undeniably an adept—neither did he say he had it, nor did he say he did not have it; he was like an ocean away from the monk from the Western Capital. Chen Ju brought this up and said, "Those Ancients; one acted as the head, the other as the tail, for sure."

Hsueh Tou's verse says,

VERSE

After Huang Ch'ao's passing, he had picked up the sword.
    What is the usefulness of an impetuous fellow? This is just a tin knife.

The great laughter after all needs an adept to understand it.
    One son is familiar with it. How many could be?

Thirty blows of the mountain cane is still a light punishment;
    Born of the same lineage, they die of the same lineage. In the morning, three thousand; in the evening, eight hundred. When someone in the eastern house dies, someone of the western house helps in the mourning. But can they bring him back to life?

To take advantage is to lose the advantage.
    He settles the case according to the facts. It is regrettable not to have been careful in the very beginning.

COMMENTARY

"After Huang Ch'ao's passing, he had picked up the sword. The great laughter needs an adept to understand it." Hsueh Tou immediately versifies this monk and Yen T'ou's great laughter. This little bit cannot be grasped by anyone in the world. But tell me, what was he laughing at? You must be an adept in order to know. In this laughter there is the provisional, there is the real; there is illumination and there is function; there is killing and there is giving life.

"Thirty blows of the mountain cane is still a light punishment." This versifies this monk later coming into the presence of Hsueh Feng: the monk was as crude as before, so Feng thereupon acted as was imperative, and hit him thirty times with his staff and drove him out. But tell me, why did he act like this? Do you want to understand this story fully? "To take the advantage is to lose the advantage."

TRANSLATORS' NOTES

a. In 874 a rebellion against the T'ang dynasty broke out, and under the leadership of Wang Hsien-chih overthrew government forces in many parts of China. Huang Ch'ao was a follower of Wang, and when the latter was killed in the fifth year of the rebellion, Huang Ch'ao took over the leadership of the rebel forces. Eventually they occupied Ch'ang An, the western capital, and slew all the members of the Imperial family who were still there. Huang Ch'ao proclaimed himself Emperor and intended to start a new dynasty, but in 881 he was finally driven out of Ch'ang An, and in 884 he was at last defeated and killed. This great rebellion, which brought about the ultimate downfall of the T'ang dynasty, is usually known as the Huang Ch'ao rebellion. Huang Ch'ao himself had earlier failed the government civil service examinations several times and had taken up salt-selling. According to legend, one day he suddenly obtained a sword which was inscribed, "Heaven gives this to Huang Ch'ao," and this inspired him to join the rebel forces of Wang Hsien-chih. In Ch'an terminology, a sword is a metaphor for *prajna,* or transcendent wisdom; Yen T'ou used the fact that the monk came from Ch'ang An to pose his question in this way. Yen T'ou died in 887, so the Huang Ch'ao rebellion was a current event.

Mahasattva Fu Expounds the Scripture

CASE

Emperor Wu of Liang requested Mahasattva Fu to expound the Diamond Cutter Scripture.[1] The Mahasattva shook the desk once, then got down off the seat.[2] Emperor Wu was astonished.[3]

Master Chih asked him, "Does Your Majesty understand?"[4] The Emperor said, "I do not understand."[5] Master Chih said, "The Mahasattva Fu has expounded the scripture."[6]

NOTES

1. Bodhidharma's brother has come. This is not unheard of in fish markets and wineshops, but in the school of the patchrobed monks, it is inappropriate. This old fellow Fu is supposedly so venerable and great, yet he acts like this.
2. He's like a comet bursting out then disappearing. He seems to be right, but is not yet really right. He doesn't bother to create any entangling complications.
3. Twice and three times he's been fooled by someone. Fu too makes him unable to get a grasp.
4. He sides with principle, not with emotion. The elbow does not bend outward. He too should be given thirty blows.
5. What a pity!
6. He too should be driven from the country. Only if Emperor Wu at that time had at once driven Master Chih out of the country along with Mahasattva Fu would he have been an adept. (Chih and Fu) are two fellows in the same pit, where the dirt is no different.

COMMENTARY

Emperor Wu, the founder of the Liang Dynasty, was of the Hsiao clan. His name was Yen and his nickname was Shu Ta. By the deeds he accomplished, he came to secure the abdication of the Ch'i Dynasty.ª After he had assumed the throne, he made new commentaries on the Five Confucian Classics, to expound them. He served Huang-Lao (Taoism) very faithfully, and his nature was most filial.

One day he thought of attaining the transmundane teaching in order to requite (his parents') toil. At this point he abandoned Taoism and served Buddhism. Then he received the Bodhisattva precepts from the Dharma Master Lou Yueh. He put on Buddhist vestments and personally expounded the Light-emitting Wisdom Scripture to recompense his parents.

At the time, the Mahasattva Master Chih, because he manifested wonders and confused people, was confined in prison. Master Chih then reproduced his body and wandered around teaching in the city. The emperor one day found out about this and was inspired. He esteemed Chih most highly. Master Chih time and again practiced protective concealment; his disappearances and appearances were incomprehensible.

At that time there was a Mahasattva in Wu Chou, dwelling on Yun Huang Mountain. He had personally planted two trees and called them the "Twin Trees." He called himself the "Future Mahasattva Shan Hui." One day he composed a letter and had a disciple present it to the emperor. At the time, the court did not accept it because he had neglected the formalities of a subject in respect to the ruler.

When the Mahasattva Fu was going to go into the city of Chin Ling (Nanking, the capital of Liang) to sell fish, at that time the emperor Wu happened to request Master Chih to expound the Diamond Cutter Scripture. Chih said, "This poor wayfarer cannot expound it, but in the market place there is a Mahasattva Fu who is able to expound the scripture." The emperor issued an imperial order to summon him to the inner palace.

Once Mahasattva Fu had arrived, he mounted the lecturing seat, shook the desk once, and then got down off the seat. At that moment, if (Wu) had pushed it over for him, he would have avoided a mess; instead he was asked by Master Chih, "Does Your Majesty understand?" The emperor said, "I do not understand." Master Chih said, "The Mahasattva has expounded the scripture thoroughly." This too is one man acting as the head and one man acting as the tail. But when Master Chih spoke in this way, did he after all see Mahasattva Fu, even in a dream? Everyone gives play to their spirits, but this one is outstanding among them. Although it is a deadly snake, if you know how to handle it, you'll still be alive. Since he was expounding the scripture, why then did he not make the general distinction into two aspects, just as ordinary lecturers say— "The substance of the Diamond is hard and solid, so that nothing can destroy it; because of its sharp function, it can smash myriad things." Explaining like this could then be called expounding the scripture. People hardly understand: the Mahasattva Fu only brought up the transcendental mainspring and briefly showed the swordpoint, to let people know the ultimate intent, directly standing it up for you like a mile-high wall. It was only appropriate that he should be subject to Master Chih's ignorance of good and bad in saying, "The Mahasattva has expounded the scripture thoroughly." Indeed, he had a good intent but didn't get a good response. It was like a cup of fine wine, which was diluted with water by Master Chih; like a bowl of soup being polluted by Master Chih with a piece of rat shit.

But tell me, granted that this is not expounding the scripture, ultimately what can you call it? The verse says,

VERSE

He does not rest this body by the Twin Trees:
> It's just because he can't hold still. How could it be possible to hide a sharp awl inside a bag?

Instead, in the land of Liang he stirs up dust.
> If he did not enter the weeds, how could we see the point? Where there is no style, there is still style.

At that time, if it weren't for old Master Chih,
> To be a thief, one does not need capital. There is a leper dragging a companion along.

He too would have been a man hastily leaving the country.
His crime should be listed on the same indictment; so I
strike.

COMMENTARY

"He does not rest this body by the Twin Trees; instead, in the
land of Liang he stirs up dust." Mahasattva Fu and that old
gap-toothed fellow (Bodhidharma) met (Emperor Wu) in the
same way. When Bodhidharma first arrived at Chin Ling and
saw Emperor Wu, the emperor asked, "What is the highest
meaning of the holy truths?" Bodhidharma said, "Empty,
without holiness." The emperor said, "Who is here in my presence?" Bodhidharma said, "I don't know." The emperor did not
understand, so Bodhidharma eventually crossed the river into
Wei. Emperor Wu mentioned this to Master Chih and asked
him about it. Chih said, "Does Your Majesty recognize this
man, or not?" The emperor said, "I do not recognize him."
Master Chih said, "This is the Mahasattva Avalokitesvara,
transmitting the seal of the Buddha-mind." The emperor felt
regret and so sent an emissary to get (Bodhidharma). Master
Chih said, "Don't tell me Your Majesty is going to send an
emissary to get him: even if everyone in the country went, he
would not return." That is why Hsueh Tou says, "At that time,
if not for Master Chih, he too would have been a man hastily
leaving the country." At the time, if it hadn't been for Master
Chih exerting energy on behalf of Mahasattva Fu, he too would
surely have been driven out of the country. Since Master Chih
was so talkative, Emperor Wu after all was fooled by him.

Hsueh Tou's intent is to say that there is no need for him to
come to the land of Liang to expound the scripture and shake
the desk. That's why he says, "Why does he not rest this body
by the Twin Trees, eating gruel and eating rice, passing the
time according to his means? Instead he comes to the land of
Liang, and comments in this way—shaking the desk once, he
immediately gets down off the seat." This is where he stirs up
dust.

If you want the marvelous, then look at the cloudy skies;
above you do not see that there is any Buddha, and below you
do not see that there are any sentient beings. If you discuss the

business of appearing in the world, you cannot avoid ashes on your head and dirt on your face, taking the non-existent and making it exist, taking the existent and making it not exist; taking right and making it wrong, taking coarse and making it fine; in the fish markets and wineshops, holding it sideways and using it upside down, making everyone understand this matter. If you do not let go in this way, then even until Maitreya is born, there will not be one or a half (who will understand). Mahasattva Fu was already dragging in mud and dripping with water; fortunately he had a sympathizer. If not for old Master Chih, he would probably have been driven out of the country. But tell me, where is he now?

TRANSLATORS' NOTES

a. Murderous fighting within the ruling Liu clan gave the local commander Hsiao Tao Cheng the chance to overthrow the Sung and set up his new Ch'i Dynasty in 479. Within fifteen years a collateral branch of the Hsiao clan had usurped the throne, leading to new strife and inner turmoil and giving an opportunity for a local commander to repeat the scenario. This man, Hsiao Yen, became Emperor Wu of the Liang Dynasty.

Yang Shan's What's Your Name?

POINTER

He overthrows the polar star and reverses the earthly axis; he captures tigers and rhinos, distinguishes dragons from snakes—one must be a lively acting fellow before he can match phrase for phrase, and correspond act to act. But since time immemorial, who could be this way? Please bring him up for me to see.

CASE

Yang Shan asked San Sheng, "What is your name?"[1]
    Sheng said, "Hui Chi."[2]
    Yang Shan said, "Hui Chi? That's me."[3]
    Sheng said, "My name is Hui Jan."[4]
    Yang Shan laughed aloud.[5]

NOTES

1. His name is about to be stolen. He brings in a thief, who ransacks his house.
2. (San Sheng) cut off (Yang Shan's) tongue; took his flag and stole his drum.
3. Each guards his own territory.
4. He steals in the noisy market place. That one and this one guard their own portion.
5. It can be said that this is the season; he spreads flowers on brocade.

COMMENTARY

San Sheng was a venerable adept in the Lin Chi succession. Since youth he possessed abilities that stood out from the crowd: he had great capacity and had great function; while still in the community, he was in full vigor, and his name was known everywhere.

Later he left Lin Chi and travelled throughout Huai Nan and Hai Chou^a; the monasteries everywhere he went all treated him as a distinguished guest. He went from the north to the south; first he went to Hsueh Feng and asked, "What does a golden carp who has passed through the net take for food?" Feng said, "Wait till you've come out of the net; then I'll tell you." Sheng said, "The teacher of fifteen hundred people doesn't even know what to say." Feng said, "My tasks as abbot are many." As Hsueh Feng was going to the temple manor, on the way he encountered some macaques, whereupon he said, "Each of the macaques is wearing an ancient mirror." San Sheng said, "For aeons it has been nameless; why do you depict it as an ancient mirror?" Feng said, "A flaw has been created." Sheng said, "The teacher of fifteen hundred people does not even know what to say." Feng said, "My fault. My tasks as abbot are many."

Later he came to Yang Shan. Shan very much admired his outstanding acuity and seated him under the bright window.^b One day an official came to call on Yang Shan. Shan asked him, "What is your official position?" He said, "I am a judge." Shan raised his whisk and said, "And can you judge this?" The official was speechless. All the people of the community made comments, but none accorded with Yang Shan's idea. At that time San Sheng was sick and staying in the Life-Prolonging Hall; Yang Shan ordered his attendant to take these words and ask him about them. Sheng said, "The Master has a problem." (Yang Shan) again ordered his attendant to ask, "What is the problem?" Sheng said, "A second offense is not permitted." Yang Shan deeply approved of this.

Pai Chang had formerly imparted his meditation brace and cushion to Huang Po, and had bequeathed his staff and whisk to Kuei Shan; Kuei Shan later gave them to Yang Shan. Since Yang Shan greatly approved of San Sheng, when one day Sheng took his leave and departed, Yang Shan took his staff and whisk to hand them over to San Sheng. Sheng said, "I already have a teacher." When Yang Shan inquired into his reason for saying this, it was that he was a true heir of Lin Chi.

When Yang Shan asked San Sheng, "What is your name?"

he could not have but known his name; why did he then go ahead and ask in this way? The reason is that an adept wants to test people to be able to know them thoroughly. He just seemed to be casually asking, "What is your name?", and spoke no further judgement or comparison. Why did San Sheng not say "Hui Jan," but instead said, "Hui Chi"? See how a man who has the eye is naturally not the same (as others). This manner of San Sheng's was still not crazy, though; he simply captured the flag and stole the drum. His meaning was beyond Yang Shan's words. These words do not fall within the scope of ordinary feelings; they are difficult to get a grasp on. The methods of such a fellow can bring people to life; that is why it is said, "He studies the living phrase—he does not study the dead phrase." If they followed ordinary feelings, then they couldn't set people at rest.

See how those men of old contemplated the Path like this: they exerted their spirits to the utmost, and only then were capable of great enlightenment. Once they were completely enlightened, when they used it, after all they appeared the same as people who were not yet enlightened. In any case, their one word or half a phrase could not fall into ordinary feelings.

San Sheng knew where Yang Shan was at, so he said to him, "My name is Hui Chi." Yang Shan wanted to take in San Sheng, but San Sheng conversely took in Yang Shan. Yang Shan was only able to make a counterattack and say, "I am Hui Chi." This is where he let go. San Sheng said. "My name is Hui Jan." This too is letting go. This is why Hsueh Tou later says, "Both gather in, both let go—which is fundamental?" With just one phrase he has completely versified it all at once.

Yang Shan laughed aloud. "Ha,ha!" There was both the provisional and the real, there was both illumination and function. Because he was crystal clear in every respect, therefore he functioned with complete freedom. This laugh was not the same as Yen T'ou's; in Yen T'ou's laugh there was poison, but in this laugh, for all eternity the pure wind blows chill.

VERSE

Both gather in, both let go—which is fundamental?
> I don't know how many of them there are. Crystal clear in every respect. I thought that there really was such a thing.

To ride a tiger always requires absolute competence.
    If you don't have the eye on your forehead and a talisman
    under your elbow, how could you get here? Ride you may,
    but I only fear you won't be able to get down. If you are
    not such a man, how could you understand such a thing?

His laughter ended, I do not know where he's gone;
    Even if you seek throughout the country for such a man,
    he would be hard to find. His words are still in our ears.
    For ever and ever there is the pure wind.

It is only fitting eternally to stir the wind of lament.
    Right now where is he? Bah! Since it is great laughter,
    why (does it) stir a piteous wind? The whole earth is
    flooded with darkness.

COMMENTARY

"Both gather in, both let go—which is fundamental?" Letting
go, alternately they act as guest and host. Yang Shan says,
"What is your name?" San Sheng says, "My name is Hui Chi."
This is both letting go. Yang Shan says, "I am Hui Chi." Sheng
says, "I am Hui Jan." This is both gathering in. In reality, this is
the action of interchange: when gathering up, everyone gathers
up; when letting go, everyone lets go. Hsueh T'ou has all at
once completely versified it. What he means to say is that if we
don't let go and gather up, if we don't interchange, then you are
you and I am I.

    The whole thing is just four characters (Hui Chi, Hui Jan):
why is there after all emergence and disappearance, spreading
out and rolling up therein? An Ancient said, "If you stand, I
then sit; if you sit, I then stand. If we both sit or both stand at
the same time, we'll both be blind men." This is both gathering, both releasing, which can be considered the fundamental
essential.

    "To ride a tiger always requires absolute competence."
When you have such a lofty manner, the highest essential of
active potential, when you want to ride, you ride; when you
want to dismount, you dismount. You can sit on the tiger's
head and also hold the tiger's tail. San Sheng and Yang Shan
both had this style.

"His laughter ended, I do not know where he's gone." Tell me, what did he laugh at? He was just like the pure wind blowing chill and severe. Why does (Hsueh Tou) after all say in the end, "It is only fitting eternally to stir the wind of lament"? This too is death without mourning; all at once he has finished adding explanations for you, but nevertheless no one in the world can bite in, and they do not know where (Yang Shan) is at. Even I do not know where he is at; do you people know?

TRANSLATORS' NOTES

a. Central eastern and southeastern China; there were many monasteries in these regions where Ch'an flourished in the late T'ang and Five Dynasties eras.
b. This means the first seat in the monks' hall, seat of the "chief monk," highest rank in the hall.

Nan Ch'uan's Circle

POINTER

There is no place to bite into: the Patriarchal Teacher's Mind Seal is formed like the works of the Iron Ox.[a] Having passed through the forest of thorns, a patchrobed monk is like a snowflake in a red hot furnace. As for piercing and penetrating on level ground, this I leave aside for the moment. Without falling into entangling ties, how will you act? To test, I cite this: look!

CASE

Nan Ch'uan, Kuei Tsung, and Ma Ku went together to pay respects to National Teacher Chung. When they got halfway there,[1] Nan Ch'uan drew a circle on the ground and said, "If you can speak, then let's go on."[2] Kuei Tsung sat down inside the circle;[3] Ma Ku curtseyed.[4] Nan Ch'uan said, "Then let's not go on."[5]

Kuei Tsung said, "What's going on in your mind?"[6]

NOTES

1. "Among three people travelling together, there must be a teacher of mine." What is so special? Still, they want to discern the truth.
2. He rouses waves where there is no wind. Still he wants people to know. He casts off a boat that's foundered on solid ground. Without posing a test, how could he discern the truth?
3. When one man strikes the cymbal, his companions join in.
4. When one man strikes the drum, all three prove able.
5. The one who can extricate himself halfway along is a good man. A good tune! An adept! An adept!

6. A lucky thing he understood him completely. At the time he should have given him a slap. Brash fellow!

COMMENTARY

At that time Ma Tsu's teaching was flourishing in Kiangsi, Shih T'ou's Way was current in Hu-Hsiang (Hunan), and National Teacher Chung's Way was influencing Ch'ang An. The latter had personally seen the Sixth Patriarch; at the time, of those in the South who held up their heads and wore horns, there was none who did not want to ascend his hall and enter his room; otherwise, they would be shamed by others.

These three old fellows wanted to go pay respects to National Teacher Chung; when they got half-way, they enacted this scenario of defeat. Nan Ch'uan said, "Then let's not go." Since they had each been able to speak, why did he instead say he wouldn't go? Tell me, what was the intention of that man of old? At that time, when he said, "Then let's not go," I would have slapped him right on the ear, to see what trick he would pull; what eternally upholds the all-embracing source is just this little bit of active essence. That is why Tz'u Ming said, "If you want to restrain him, just grab the rein and yank." Hit and he turns, like pushing down a gourd on the water. Many people say that (Nan Ch'uan's) words are words of disagreement, but they are far from knowing that in this matter, when you get to the ultimate point, it is necessary to leave the mud, get out of the water, draw out the wedges, and pull out the nails. If you make an intellectual interpretation, then you've missed it. The Ancients could turn and shift well; at this point they could not be otherwise—there must be killing and giving life: see how one of them sat inside the circle, and one curtseyed. That too was very good. Nan Ch'uan said, "Then let's not go." Kuei Tsung said, "What is going on in your mind?" Brash fellow! He too goes on like this. His whole idea was that he wanted to test Nan Ch'uan. Nan Ch'uan always said, "Call it thusness, and already it has changed." Nan Ch'uan, Kuei Tsung, and Ma Ku—after all they were people of one house. One holds, one releases; one kills, one enlivens: undeniably they are exceptional.

Hueh Tou's verse says:

VERSE

You Chi's arrow shoots the monkey:
Who would dare to advance on the road facing him?Whenever he hits, he is marvelous; he hits the mark before he shoots.

Circling the tree, how exceedingly direct!
Without attaining mastery, how could one presume to be thus? North, south, east, west—one family style. They have already been going around for a long time.

A thousand and ten thousand—
Plentiful as hemp and millet. A pack of wild fox spirits. What about Nan Ch'uan?

Who has ever hit the mark?
One or a half. Not even one. Even one would still be no use.

Calling them together, he beckons them, "Come, let's go back;"
They're a bunch of fellows playing with a lump of mud. This is not as good as having gone back; then they would have gotten somewhere.

He stops climbing on the road of Ts'ao Ch'i.
Too much trouble. It seems to me that he is not a member of Ts'ao Ch'i's school. Level off the lowest of places, and there is too much; view the highest of places, and there is not enough.

(Hsueh Tou) also said, "The road of Ts'ao Ch'i is level and even; why stop climbing?"
Not only Nan Ch'uan extricates himself halfway along; Hsueh Tou also extricates himself halfway along. Even a good thing is not as good as nothing. Hsueh Tou too suffers from this kind of illness and pain.

COMMENTARY

"You Chi's arrow shoots the monkey; circling the tree, how exceedingly direct!" You Chi was a man of Ch'u times; his surname was Yang, his name was Shu and his nickname was

You Chi. Once when King Chuang of Ch'u went out hunting, he saw a white monkey and had someone shoot it. That monkey grabbed the arrow and played with it. The King ordered his entourage of courtiers to shoot it, but none could hit it. The King then asked his courtiers, and they said to him, "The man You Chi is a good shot." So he ordered him to shoot it. As You Chi drew his bow, the monkey immediately hugged the tree and howled piteously. When the arrow was shot, the monkey went around the tree to avoid it. The arrow also circled the tree, and struck and killed the monkey. This was a supernatural arrow. Why does Hsueh Tou say it was exceedingly direct? If it had been too direct, it wouldn't have hit; since it went around the tree, why instead does Hsueh Tou say it was exceedingly direct? Hsueh Tou borrows the idea and indeed uses it well. This even appears in the *Ch'un Ch'iu:*[b] some people say that "circling the tree" is the circle; if they really think so, they do not know the basic import of the words— they do not know where the directness is. These three old fellows are on different roads but return to the same place. They are uniformly and equally exceedingly direct. If you know where they're going, then you are free in all directions without leaving your heart. A hundred rivers flow separately but alike return to the great sea. That is why Nan Ch'uan said, "Then let's not go." If you look at this with the true eye of a patchrobed monk, this is just giving play to the spirit: but if you call it giving play to the spirit, then it is not giving play to the spirit. My late Master Wu Tsu said, "Those three men were absorbed in the Lamp of Wisdom, absorbed in the King of Adornment." Although (Ma Ku) curtseyed in this way, he never understood it as curtseying; although (Nan Ch'uan) made a circle, he never understood it as a circle. Without understanding in this way, then how will you understand? Hsueh Tou says, "A thousand and ten thousand—who has ever hit the mark?" How many could there be who hit the mark a hundred times out of a hundred?

"Calling them together, he beckons them, 'Come, let us go back.'" This is versifying Nan Ch'uan's saying, "Then let's not go on." Nan Ch'uan did not go on from here, so it is said, "He stops climbing on the road of Ts'ao Ch'i." He destroys the forest of thorns. Hsueh Tou cannot hold still, and again says, "The road of Ts'ao Ch'i is level and even; why stop climbing?"

The road of Ts'ao Ch'i is dustless and trackless, openly exposed, naked and clean, level, even, and smooth: why, after all, stop climbing? Each of you should observe your own footsteps.

TRANSLATORS' NOTES

a. See Translators' Note a, Case 38.
b. The *Ch'un Ch'iu* is a classic book of historical annals of the state of Lu, said to have been composed by Confucius himself, covering the period 722–481 B.C., before the first unification of China. This eminent chronicle became a model for later histories.

Biographical Supplement

The order of the biographies is as follows:

LINEAGE OF MASTERS APPEARING IN VOLUME II

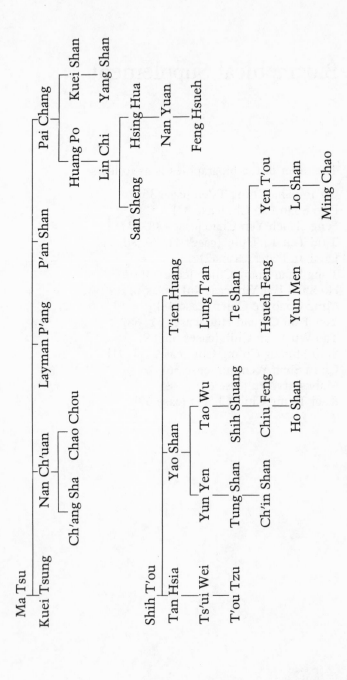

CHING TS'EN, 'Great Master Chao Hsien' of Ch'ang Sha in Hunan (n.d.)

CASE 36

(Known as Ch'ang Sha, he was a distinguished successor of Nan Ch'uan; the following is taken from *Ching Te Ch'uan Teng Lu* 10)

He first dwelt at the Deer Park, where he was the first generation; after that he dwelt in no fixed abode, but just went along with circumstances and expounded the Dharma as was appropriate to the occasion. At the time he was called 'The Teacher of Ch'ang Sha.'

> In the hall he said, If I were to thoroughly uphold the teaching of our sect, there would be weeds a fathom deep in the teaching hall; (but) I am unable to avoid facing all of you people and saying that the entire cosmos is the eye of a monk; the entire cosmos is the whole body of a monk; the entire cosmos is one's own light; the entire cosmos lies within one's own light; in the whole cosmos there is no one who is not oneself.
>
> I always tell you people that the Buddhas of the triple world, the cosmos, and the mass of living beings, are the light of great perfect wisdom. When the light has not yet shone forth, where can you people turn to become intimately acquainted with it? Before the light shines forth, there isn't even any news of Buddhas or sentient beings; where do we get the mountains, rivers, and earth?

At that time a monk asked, "What is the monk's eye?"

The master said, "Never, ever can one depart from it; (those who) attain Buddhahood and become patriarchs cannot depart from it; the six paths of transmigration cannot depart from it."

The monk said, "What is it that they cannot depart from?"

The master said, "In daytime, seeing the sun; at night, seeing stars."

The monk said, "I don't understand."

The master said, "Marvelous towering mountains, their color blue upon blue."

A monk asked, "Who is the teacher of all Buddhas?"

The master said, "By whom has he been concealed ever since beginningless aeons?"

A monk asked, "How is it when the student does not depend on the ground?"

The master said, "Where will you rest your body and live?"

He asked, "Then how is it when he does depend on the ground?"

The master said, "Drag this corpse away!"

He asked, "What are 'different kinds'?"

The master said, "A foot is short, an inch is long."

The master sent a monk to ask Teacher Hui, a former fellow student, "How is it after the teacher had seen Nan Ch'uan?" Hui was silent. The monk said, "How about before the teacher had seen Nan Ch'uan?" Hui said, "There could not be another besides." The monk returned and quoted this to the master. The master spoke a verse, saying,

> The unmoving man atop the hundred-foot pole:
> Though he has gained entry, he is not yet real.
> Atop the hundred-foot pole, he should step
>   forward—
> The whole universe in the ten directions is his
>   whole body.

The monk then asked, "Atop the hundred-foot pole, how to advance?" The master said, "Mountains of Liang, rivers of Li." The monk said, "I don't understand." The master said, "The whole country is under the imperial sway."

(Many more sayings are attributed to Ch'ang Sha; he had two enlightened successors.)

PAO CHI of P'an Shan in Yu Chou (n.d.)
CASE 37

(P'an Shan was a successor of Ma Tsu; his abode was in northern China, near modern-day North Korea. He was one of the few early Ch'an masters to teach in this region. Of his two successors, P'u Hua is the only one about whom anything is known; P'u Hua later assisted the great Lin Chi in his teaching. The story of P'an Shan's enlightenment is given in *Wu Teng Hui Yuan* 3)

As the master was walking through a market place, he saw a customer who was buying some pork say to the butcher, "Cut me a pound of the fine stuff." The butcher put down his cleaver, folded his hands and said, "Inspector, which isn't fine?" At this, the master had insight.

Again one day when he had gone out of the monastery, he saw people in mourning, singing and ringing bells: "The red disc inevitably sinks into the west; we don't know where the ghost will go." Inside an enclosure, a filial son was crying, "Alas! Alas!" The master's body and mind leaped; he returned and told Ma Tsu about it. Ma Tsu gave him his seal of approval.

(The saying which forms case 37 is taken from a longer sermon of P'an Shan, other parts of which are repeatedly quoted in Yuan Wu's commentaries throughout the text. The following version is from *Ching Te Ch'uan Teng Lu* 7; given in parentheses are significant variants from the version given in *Tsu T'ang Chi* 15:)

If there is no concern in the mind, myriad forms are unborn. When the mind is devoid of subtle activity, where can a trace of dust remain? The Way fundamentally has no substance; because of speaking, a name is established. The Way fundamentally has no name; because of naming, an epithet is found. If you say the very mind itself is identical to Buddha, still people these days have not yet entered the profound subtlety; if you say it is not mind, not Buddha, this is still the ultimate example of pointing to the traces. The one road going upwards, the thousand sages did not transmit; students toil over forms like monkeys grasping at reflections. The Great Way has no middle; who then goes forward or back? The eternal void is without bound; how could it be measured? Since the void is like this, how could the Way be spoken of? The mind-moon solitary and full, its light engulfs myriad forms: the light is not shining on objects, and the objects also do not remain; when light and objects are both gone, then what thing is this? Ch'an worthies, it is like hurling a sword into the sky; do not speak of reaching or not reaching: then the wheel of the void is without a trace, the sword's blade is without a flaw. If you can be like this, mind and mental conditions are without knowledge. The whole mind is identical to Buddha; the whole Buddha is identical to man. When mind and Buddha are not different, then this is the Way. Ch'an worthies should study the middle path: like the earth supporting a mountain, unaware of the mountain's steep height; like a stone containing a gem, without knowing the gem is flawless. If you can be like this, this is called Leaving Home. Thus the Guide said, "Things fundamentally do not hinder each other; the three times are also the same." A nondoing, unconcerned man still has the problem of the golden chains; therefore an Ancient said, "The spiritual source shines alone; the Path is fundamentally birthless." Great wisdom is not clarity; the true void is trackless. In true thusness, "ordinary" and "holy" are all dream talk; "Buddha" and "Nirvana" are both excess words. Ch'an worthies, you must see for yourselves; no one can substitute for you. There is nothing in the triple world; where can mind be found? The four elements are originally void; how can a Buddha abide? The turning potential doesn't move (The oracle doesn't move); it is silent and rootless (it is silent and speechless). Once it is presented right to your face, there is nothing else. Farewell.

YEN CHAO of Feng Hsueh (896—973)
CASES 38, 61

Feng Hsueh originally studied Confucianism; he sat for the civil service examination once, but failed. After that, he abandoned home to become a Buddhist. First he studied the 'stopping and observing' methods of T'ien T'ai Buddhist meditation; he then turned to Ch'an. He finally succeeded to Nan Yuan Hui Yung, a third generation Lin Chi master. He first taught at Feng Hsueh in Ju Chou (in Honan), at the request of the community there. He spent a summer in the Yamen at Ying Chou because the local army had revolted and the area was in danger. Later he was requested to return to Ju Chou, where he spent the last twenty-two years of his life teaching a congregation of over a hundred students.

Hsing Nien of Shou Shan, who was a latecomer to Feng Hsueh's community, served as the receiver of guests there: according to the *Wu Teng Hui Yuan* 11, one day as he was standing by, Hsueh wept and said to him, "Unfortunately, the way of Lin Chi, having reached me, is about to fall to the ground." Hsing Nien said, "As you look upon this whole community, is there no one at all?" Hsueh said, "There are many who are intelligent, but few who perceive nature." Nien said, "What about me?" Hsueh said, "Though I've had hopes for you for a long time, I still fear you are addicted to this sutra and can't let it go." (Hsing Nien constantly recited the Lotus Sutra to himself.) Nien said, "This too should be served: but I beg to hear its essence." Hsueh then went into the hall and cited the World Honored One's looking over the great crowd with his blue lotus eyes, then said, "Tell me, at that time, what did he say? If you say he spoke without speaking, this is still burying that former sage. Tell me, what did he say?" Nien then shook out his sleeves and left.

Hsueh threw down his staff and returned to the abbot's room; his attendant followed him and asked for further instruction, saying, "Why did Nien not answer you, master?" Hsueh said, "Nien understands."

The next day as Hsing Nien went along with gardener Chen to inquire (into the master's health), Hsueh asked Chen, "What is the World Honored One's unspoken speech?" Chen said, "A dove calling in a tree." Hsueh said, "Why do you make so much abundance of folly? Why don't you thoroughly investigate the spoken phrases?" He also asked Hsing Nien about it; Nien said, "Activity upholds the ancient road, without falling into passivity." Feng said to Chen, "Why don't you observe Nien's comment?"

After Hsing Nien had received Feng Hsueh's seal of approval, he obliterated his tracks and concealed his light.

(Shou Shan Hsing Nien (925-992) later appeared to teach, as the first patriarch of Shou Shan; this was in the beginning of the Sung dynasty, when the country was more stable. Shou Shan had sixteen successors, among whom was Fen Yang Shan Chao (947-1024), said to be an originator of poetic commentary to ancient *kung an*. Fen Yang is said to have seen seventy-one teachers, and attempted to synthesize the various illustrative schemes of the Ch'an schools; the Lin Chi branch of Ch'an flourished greatly with his successors and descendants, becoming the dominant school of Buddhism in China.)

TA T'UNG of Mt. T'ou Tzu (845—914)
CASES 41, 79, 80, 91

(The following is taken from the *Ching Te Ch'uan Teng Lu* 15)

He was a man from Huai Ning in Shu Chou (in Anhui); his surname was Liu. He left home at an early age . . . . He first practiced breath-contemplation; next he investigated the Hua Yen teachings and discovered the ocean of nature. He visited the Dharma assembly on Mt. Ts'ui Wei and was suddenly awakened to Ts'ui Wei's source meaning. (This is told in the *Ch'uan Teng Lu* 14:)

T'ou Tzu asked Ts'ui Wei, "I wonder, when the Second Patriarch first saw Bodhidharma, what was really attained?" Ts'ui Wei said, "What is attained right now when you see me?" One day as Ts'ui Wei was walking inside the Dharma Hall, T'ou Tzu approached him, bowed, and asked, "Teacher, how do you show people the secret message of the coming from the West?" Ts'ui Wei stopped for a moment. T'ou Tzu again said, "Please, Teacher, instruct me." Ts'ui Wei said, "Do you want a second ladleful of foul water besides?" T'ou Tzu bowed in thanks and withdrew.

(After this) T'ou Tzu wandered all over as he pleased, returning to frequent his native territory. He concealed himself on Mt. T'ou Tzu (which is in Shu Chou), built a grass hut, and lived there.

(The following story leads up to the dialogue between Chao Chou and T'ou Tzu that makes the Main Case 41:) One day Master Shen of Chao Chou came to (a nearby district); T'ou Tzu too had come down from the mountain that day. They encountered each other on the road without recognizing each other. Chao Chou privately asked a lay gentleman and found out it was T'ou Tzu. Then he turned back (to go after him). He asked, "Aren't you the master of Mt. T'ou Tzu?" T'ou Tzu said, "I beg you for a coin for the tea and salt tax." Chao Chou then went up onto Mt. T'ou Tzu first and sat there in his hut, (waiting for T'ou Tzu to return.) Later T'ou Tzu returned to his hermitage, bringing along a jar of oil. Chao Chou said, "I've long heard of T'ou Tzu, but now that I've come here I just see an old man selling oil." T'ou Tzu said, "You just see an old man selling oil, but you don't know T'ou Tzu." Chao Chou

said, "What is T'ou Tzu?" T'ou Tzu said, "Oily oil." Chao
Chou said, "How is it when gaining life amidst death?" T'ou
Tzu said, "One must not go by night; one must get there by
daylight." Chao Chou said, "I'm a swindler, yet you swindled
me."

Henceforward T'ou Tzu's Path was heard of all over the
country, and "cloud and rain" folk (traveling Ch'an students)
flocked to him. The master told the assembly, "All of you have
come here trying to find fresh new sayings and beautiful verses.
I am an old man whose strength has dwindled, my way of
talking is slow and blunt. If you question me, I'll follow you
and give my reply. I have no hidden marvels that can be conveyed to you. . . .Here there is nothing that can be given to you,
there is no outside or inside that can be related to you. Do all of
you realize this?" . . .The master lived on Mt. T'ou Tzu for
over thirty years. He dealt with and aroused those who came
seeking instruction who constantly filled his room.

The Huang Chao revolt broke out in 881 and there was
chaos throughout the country. A madman came up the mountain carrying a blade; he asked T'ou Tzu what he was living
there for, so the master expounded the Dharma in accordance
with the situation to the man. When he heard this, the man
bowed and submitted; then he stripped off his clothes and gave
them to T'ou Tzu and went away.

In 914 the master showed a slight illness: the congregation
wanted to call a doctor, but the master told them, "The activity of the four elements is a continual process of assembly and
dissolution. Don't you worry: I'll preserve myself." When he
finished talking, he sat cross-legged and died.

LAYMAN P'ANG (8–9 cent.)
CASE 42

(Layman P'ang succeeded to both Shih T'ou and Ma Tsu, the
foremost teachers of the eighth century. He had been a minor
civil official, but later he took all his wealth and sank it in a
river. His family of a wife, son, and daughter split up, and he
went from place to place with his daughter, weaving bamboo
baskets and selling them to make a living. In his travels he

visited many of the Ch'an masters who had succeeded to Ma Tsu. The following account is excerpted from *Ching Te Ch'uan Teng Lu* 8)

His name was Tao Hsuan: in the world, Confucianism was his business; yet the layman somewhat understood the toil of passion, and aspired to seek the real truth. In the latter 780's he visited Master Shih T'ou; he forgot the words and comprehended the inner meaning. He also was a friend of Ch'an Master Tan Hsia (a successor of Shih T'ou).

One day Shih T'ou asked him, "Since you've seen me, how are your daily affairs?" He responded, "If you ask about my daily affairs, I have no way to open my mouth." He also presented a verse which said,

> In my daily affairs there's nothing different;
> Only I myself am in harmony.
> Nothing do I grasp or reject,
> Nowhere do I insist or turn away.
> Who regards crimson and purple as honorable?
> The hills and mountains are void of any dust.
> Supernatural powers and their marvelous function—
> Fetching water and carrying firewood.

Shih T'ou approved of this; he said, "Will you be a monk or a layman?" The layman said, "I want to follow my wish," and after all did not shave his head or wear the dark (garment of a monk).

Later he went to Kiangsi and asked Ma Tsu, "Who is he who is not the companion of myriad things?" Tsu said, "When you swallow all the water of the West River in one gulp, then I'll tell you." At these words the layman suddenly apprehended the abstruse essence; subsequently he stayed to learn for two years. He had a verse which said,

> I have a son who does not marry
> And a daughter who does not wed:
> The whole family gathered 'round,
> Together we speak birthless talk.

Henceforth his eloquence was swift; he was heard of everywhere. . . . He had three hundred and more poems which circulated in the world.

LIANG CHIEH of Tung Shan (806—869)
CASE 43

(The following account is taken from *Wu Teng Hui Yuan* 13)

In youth he followed a teacher and recited the Perfection of Wisdom Heart Sutra; coming to where it says, 'There is no eye, ear, nose, tongue, body, or mind,' he suddenly felt his face and asked the teacher, "I have eyes, ears, nose, tongue, and so forth; why does the sutra say there are none?" The teacher was surprised at this and said, "I am not your teacher." Then he directed him to go to Mt. Wu Hsieh (in Chekiang) to pay obeisance to Ch'an master (Ling) Mo (746–818; reckoned as one of Ma Tsu's successors, he was actually enlightened under Shih T'ou and was his attendant for twenty years), by whom he had his head shaved. At twenty-one he went to Sung Shan and received the precepts in full.

Travelling around, he first called on Nan Ch'uan; as it happened, it was the anniversary of Ma Tsu's death, so they were preparing a ceremonial feast. Ch'uan asked the community, "Tomorrow we will set out a feast for Ma Tsu; do you think Ma Tsu will come, or not?" No one replied; the master (Tung Shan) came forth and answered, "If he has a companion, he'll come." Ch'uan said, "Though this lad is young, he is quite suitable for carving and polishing." The master said, "Teacher, don't oppress a freeman (Liang, Tung Shan's personal name) and make him a slave." (The *Tsu T'ang Chi* says that after this he began to be known as an adept.)

Next he called on Kuei Shan and asked, "I recently have heard that the National Teacher Chung of Nan Yang had a saying about inanimate objects expounding the Dharma, but I have not thoroughly comprehended its subtlety." Kuei Shan said, "Do you not remember it?" The master said, "I remember." Kuei Shan said, "Try to recite it for me." The master then recited, "A monk asked, 'What is the mind of an ancient Buddha?' The National Teacher said, 'Walls, tiles, and pebbles.' The monk said, 'Aren't walls, tiles, and pebbles inanimate?' The National Teacher said, 'That's right.' The monk said, 'And can they expound the Dharma, or not?' The National Teacher said, 'They are always expounding it clearly, without interruption.' The monk said, 'Why don't I hear it?' The National Teacher said, 'You yourself don't hear it, but you shouldn't hinder the one who does hear it.' The monk said, 'Who can hear it?' The National Teacher said, 'All the saints can hear it.' The monk said, 'Can you hear it too, Master?' The National Teacher said, 'I don't hear it.' The monk said, 'Since you don't hear it, how do you know that inanimate objects can expound the Dharma?' The National Teacher said, 'It's lucky I don't hear it; if I heard it, then I'd be equal to the saints and you wouldn't hear me expound the Dharma.' The monk said, 'Then sentient beings have no part in it.' The National Teacher said, 'I explain for sentient beings, not for the saints.' The monk said, 'How are sentient beings after they have heard it?' The National Teacher said, 'Then they are not sentient beings.' The monk said, 'What scripture is the "inanimate expounding the Dharma"based on?' The National Teacher said, 'Obviously if the words do not accord with the classics, it is not the talk of a gentleman: you have not read how the Avatamsaka Sutra says, "Lands expound it, sentient beings expound it, everything in the three times expounds it"?'"

When the master had finished reciting, Kuei Shan said, "I too have something here, but a suitable man is hard to come across." The master said, "I'm still not clear; please point it out to me." Kuei Shan raised his whisk and said, "Do you understand?" The master said, "I don't understand. Please explain." Kuei Shan said, "The mouth born of my father and mother will never explain it to you." The master said, "Is there another who sought the Way in the same time as you?" Kuei Shan said, "From here go to Yu district in Li Leng, to where there is a row of stone grottoes; there is a man of the Way there, Yun Yen; if you can pull out the weeds to find his way, he will be of value to you." The master said, "How is this man?" Kuei Shan said, "He once asked me, 'When I want to serve you, how can I do so?' I told him, 'You must just absolutely cut off all leakage before you can.' He said, 'And would I be able to not go against your teaching or not?' I said, 'Above all, don't say that I'm here.'"

The master took leave of Kuei Shan and went right to Yun Yen; having quoted the preceding incident, he asked, "Who can hear inanimate objects expounding the Dharma?" Yun Yen said, "The inanimate can hear it." The master said, "Can you hear it, teacher?" Yun Yen said, "If I heard, you would not hear my expounding of the Dharma." The master said, "Why wouldn't I hear?" Yen raised his whisk and said, "Do you hear?" The master said, "No." Yen said, "You do not even hear my expounding of the Dharma; how could you hear the inanimate expounding the Dharma?" The master said, "What scripture contains the inanimate expounding the Dharma?" Yen said, "Haven't you read how the Amitabha Sutra says, 'Rivers, birds, trees, and forests all commemorate Buddha and Dharma.'" At this the master had insight; thereupon he uttered a verse:

> *How wonderful! How wonderful!*
> *The inanimate expounding of Dharma is inconceivable;*
> *If you use your ears to listen, you'll never understand—*
> *Only when you hear in your eyes will you know.*

The master asked Yun Yen, "I have leftover habits which are not yet exhausted." Yun Yen said, "What have you ever done?" The master said, "I have not even practiced the holy truths." Yen said, "And do you rejoice, or not?" The master said, "I am not without joy; it is like finding a bright jewel in a dungheap."

When he was about to go, he asked Yun Yen, "After your death, if someone should suddenly ask me if I can depict your true likeness, how shall I answer?" Yen remained silent for a good while, then said, "Just this is it." The master was sunk in contemplation; Yen said, "Reverend Chieh, now that you have taken up this matter, you must be very careful and thoroughgoing."

The master still had some doubt; later, as he was crossing a river, he saw his reflection and was greatly awakened to the inner meaning of what had happened before. He made a verse which said,

> *Just avoid seeking from others,*
> *Or you will be far estranged from yourself.*
> *I now go on alone; I meet Him everywhere—*
> *He is now just I, but I now am not He:*
> *One must understand in this way*
> *In order to unite with thusness.*

From the end of the Ta Chung era (847–859) of T'ang, the master received and guided students at Hsin Feng Mountain; after this, he caused the teaching to flourish at Tung Mountain (Tung Shan) in Kao An in Yu Chiang (in Kiangsi). He provisionally opened up the five ranks, and skillfully handled the three potentials (high, middling, low); he greatly opened up the One Sound, and widely spread it through the myriad classes. He drew his precious sword sideways and cut off the forest of various views: his wondrous harmony spread widely, cutting off myriad rationalizations.

He also found Ts'ao Shan, who was deeply enlightened into the real essence, and wonderfully extolled the felicitous way, the harmony of the ways of lord and vassal, biased and true interdepending. Because of this the mystic breeze of the Tung succession spread throughout the land. Therefore, the masters of Ch'an everywhere all esteemed it and called it the Ts'ao-Tung Sect.

(Tung Shan had twenty-six successors; among them, Tao Ying of Yun Chu (d. 903) was one of the greatest masters of the time, who led a community of fifteen hundred people and produced twenty-eight enlightened disciples. Su Shan K'uang Jen (n.d.) was another distinguished successor to Tung Shan, with twenty enlightened disciples. The most enduring line of the Tung succession was that which came down through Yun Chu; he and Hsueh Feng, who is said to have called on Tung Shan nine times, were the foremost masters of their age in southeastern and southern China. The Ts'ao Tung sect trickled down in China until the seventeenth century; it was transmitted to Japan in the thirteenth century, over three hundred years after the founders, and still continues there in a modified form until present times.)

WU YIN of Ho Shan (—960)
CASE 44

(The following is from the Ching Te Ch'uan Teng Lu 17)

The master was a man from Fu Chou; his surname was Wu. At age seven he left home under the Great Master Hsueh Feng; when he came of age he was ordained.

The master travelled around till he come to Chün Yang and visited Chiu Feng. Feng permitted the master to enter his private room. One day Feng said to him, "You have come from far, far away to join the assembly. Have you seen any realm that can be cultivated? What shortcut can you get out by?" The master replied, "In the dark empty clearing, the blind are blind of themselves." At first Chiu Feng didn't approve: because of this the master discovered his intent and suddenly forgot his knowledge and views.

Previously the master had received an invitation to stay at Great Wisdom Temple on Ho Shan in Chi Chou (in Kiangsi). There students flocked around him. The master imparted ten booklets of admonitions which were received joyously all over. All said that Ho Shan was a suitable standard for the communities of monks.

Around this time the Li Clan (in power) south of the (Yangtse) River summoned the master. He was asked, "Where have you come from, Teacher?" The master said, "From Ho Shan." "Where is the mountain?" The master said, "The man has come for an audience at the Imperial Palace, but the mountain has never moved." The Lord esteemed him and ordered him to dwell at Lucky Light Temple in Yang Chou. The master requested (to be allowed) to go back into the mountains.

In 960 the master showed a slight illness. He ordered his attendants to open up the abbot's quarters and assemble everyone there. He bade them farewell saying, "Hereafter students won't know Ho Shan: better get acquainted right now. Take care of yourselves!"

MING CHAO TE CHIEN (n.d.)
CASE 48

(The following account is from *Ching Te Ch'uan Teng Lu* 23)

He received the seal and testimonial of Lo Shan (a successor of Yen T'ou). He did not linger in one corner (but) powerfully extolled the mystic teaching. All the elders were in awe of his genius; there were rarely any latecoming students who dared to confront his 'swordpoint.'

When the master was in the great hall of Chao Ch'ing in Ch'uan Chou (in Fukien), he pointed to a wall painting and asked a monk, "What spirit is that?" (The monk) said, "The good spirit who guards the Dharma." The master said, "Where did it go at the time of the persecution?" The monk had no reply.

The master then had the monk go ask attendant Yen. Yen said, "In what aeon did you meet with this calamity?" The monk returned and quoted this to the master; the master said, "Even if attendant Yen later on gathers a following of a thousand people, what would be the use?" The monk then bowed and asked the master for an alternate saying; the master said, "Where did it go?"

Elder Ch'ing brought up the story of Yang Shan sticking the hoe in the ground and asked the master, "Was the Ancient's meaning where he folded his hands, or is the meaning where he stuck the hoe in the ground?" The master said, "Elder Ch'ing!" Ch'ing responded; the master said, "Have you ever seen Yang Shan even in a dream?" Ch'ing said, "I don't want a comment; I just want you to discuss it." The master said, "If you want discussion, there are fifteen hundred old teachers in the hall."

The master came to Shuang Yen; the elder of Shuang Yen observed the master's appearance, then said, "I will pose a question to ask you; if you can speak, then I will abandon this temple; if you cannot speak, then I won't abandon it. The Diamond Sutra says, 'All Buddhas and all the Buddhas' teachings come forth from this sutra.' Tell me, who expounds this sutra?" The master said, "Putting 'expounding' and 'not expounding' aside for the moment, just what do you call 'this sutra'?" Shuang Yen had no reply. The master cited the sutra, saying, "All wise ones and sages rely on the uncontrived way, yet there are distinctions; this is because the uncontrived way is the ultimate law—on what basis are there distinctions? But are distinctions faults or not? If they're faults, all wise ones and sages have faults; if they're not faults, just what is to be called 'distinctions'?" Shuang Yen again had nothing to say. The master said, "What Hsueh Feng said."

When the master was in Chih Che temple in Wu Chou (in Chekiang), he sat in the first seat (as a 'head monk'). He never would take clean water. The monk who was superintendent of affairs asked him, "Why are you not conscious of defilement, that you won't take clean water?" The master got down from the platform, picked up the pure water pitcher, and said, "This is pure." The superintendent said nothing; the master then broke the water pitcher. Henceforth the master's repute in the Way spread afar.

The congregation on Mt. Ming Chou (also in Wu Chou, Chekiang) asked him to abide there and open up the teaching. Ch'an folk from all quarters filled the halls and rooms.

Someone asked, "Who can face the smokeless fire?"

The master said, "One who isn't anxious for his eyebrows."

He asked, "Can you face it, Master?"

The master said, "Tell me, how many eyebrow hairs do I have left?"

A certain monk who had been in the master's audience took his leave and went to live in a hut for a year. Later he came back and paid obeisance; he said, "A man of old said 'If you haven't met for three days, do not look upon someone as before.'" The master then exposed his chest and said, "Tell me, how many hairs do I have on my chest?" The monk had no reply. The master then asked, "When did you leave your hut?" He said, "This morning." The master said, "When you came, to whom did you give your broken-legged pot?" The monk again had nothing to say. The master then shouted him out.

(The master dwelt on Ming Chao for forty years, and 'his words were circulated everywhere.' He had five enlightened successors.)

CH'UAN HUO of Yen T'ou (827—887)
CASES 51, 66

(Yen T'ou was a successor of Te Shan and "brother" of Hsueh Feng: see Cases 5, 21, and 51. The following account is from the *Ching Te Ch'uan Teng Lu* 16)

The master was a man of Ch'uan Chou (in Hopei); his surname was K'o. In his youth he paid homage to Master Yi of (the district town) Ch'ing Yuan and had his head shaved. He went to Pao Shou Temple in (the capital) Ch'ang An and was ordained. He studied all the sections of the Sutras and Vinaya Texts.

Yen T'ou made the rounds of the Ch'an monasteries with Hsueh Feng I Ts'un and Ch'in Shan Wen Sui as his companions. From Mt. Ta Tz'u in Yü Hang he made his way to Lin Chi, but it was just after Lin Chi himself had died. Then he visited Yang Shan. As soon as he entered the gate, Yen T'ou picked up his sitting mat and said, "Teacher!" Yang Shan took his whisk and made as if to hold it up. T'ou said, "An undeniable expert."

Later Yen T'ou called on Te Shan: holding his sitting mat, he went into the Dharma Hall and looked up (at Te Shan). Te Shan said, "Well?" T'ou snorted at him. Shan said, "Where was my fault?" T'ou said, "A doubled case," then left the hall. Shan said, "This master looks a little like a foot-travelling man." The next day when Yen T'ou went up to inquire after him, Te Shan said, "Didn't you just arrive here yesterday, Reverend?" T'ou said, "That's right." Shan said, "Where did you learn this empty-headedness?" T'ou said, "I never deceive myself." Shan said, "After this you shouldn't turn your back on me." Another time Yen T'ou went to visit Te Shan: entering the abbot's quarters, T'ou contorted his body and asked, "Ordinary or sage?" Te Shan shouted, and Yen T'ou bowed in homage. (Further incidents involving Yen T'ou, Hsueh Feng and Te Shan are contained in the Commentary to Case 51.)

Yen T'ou said, "The intent of my teaching is like a poison-smeared drum: one beat and all who hear it, near and far, perish."

Later whenever anyone asked about Buddha, asked about Dharma, asked about Tao, or asked about Ch'an, Yen T'ou would always sigh.

During the 880's the central plain (i.e., the area around the capital, the heart of the realm) was infested with plundering armies: the master's congregation all fled the area. Yen T'ou himself (remained) sitting solemn and calm. One day bandits came in force. Accusing the master of not offering them any gifts, they slashed him with their blades. His countenance calm and collected, the master gave a loud shout, then died. The sound could be heard for several dozen miles.

YUAN CHIH of Tao Wu Shan (768—835)
CASES 55, 89

(The following is from the Ching Te Ch'uan Teng Lu 14)

He was originally from Hai Hun in Yü Chang (modern Nan Ch'ang); his surname was Chang. At an early age he received instruction from Master Nie'h-p'an and was ordained. He joined Yao Shan's Dharma assembly and gained intimate accord with the Mind Seal. One day Yao Shan asked him, "Where are you coming from?" Tao Wu said, "From wandering in the mountains." Yao Shan said, "Speak quickly without leaving from this room." Tao Wu said, "The ravens on the mountain are white as snow; the fish swimming in the pond are hurrying ceaselessly."

Tao Wu and Yun Yen were attending Yao Shan. Yao Shan said, "Better not speak where your wisdom doesn't reach. If you do, then horns sprout on your head. What about it, Ascetic Chih?" Tao Wu immediately left. Yun Yen asked Yao Shan, "Why did Elder Brother Chih not answer you, Teacher?" Yao Shan said, "I have a back ache today—(despite his leaving,) he does understand: go ask him." Yun Yen immediately went and asked Tao Wu, "Why didn't you reply to our Teacher, Elder Brother?" Tao Wu said, "Go back and ask our Teacher."

When Yun Yen was about to die, he sent someone to deliver his farewell letter to Tao Wu. Tao Wu opened it, glanced through it and said, "Yun Yen knows no shame: I shouldn't have spoken to him that time. Nevertheless, in essence he was a (faithful) 'son' who didn't go against Yao Shan."

Yun Yen asked, "What is your family style, Elder Brother?" Tao Wu said, "What would be the use of having you point it out?"

(Ho was asked,) "What is the place to apply effort in these times?" Tao Wu said, "If a thousand people call you, and you don't turn your head, only then will you have some small portion (of attainment.)"

He was asked, "What is your family style, Teacher?" Tao Wu got down from the meditation seat and curtseyed saying, "Thanks for coming from so far away."

In 835 Tao Wu showed sickness: he was in pain. The monks of his congregation came to offer condolences and inquire about his health. Tao Wu said, "There is an experience which is not repaid: do you realize that?" The congregation were all sorrowful. When he was about to go, Tao Wu said to them. "I am crossing over to the west, but Principle has no eastward movement." As he finished speaking, he showed the stillness of death.

CH'ING CHU of Shih Shuang Shan
(807—889)
CASES 55, 91

(The following is taken from the *Ching Te Ch'uan Teng Lu* 15)

He was originally from Hsin Kan in Lu Ling (in Kiangsi); his surname was Ch'en. At age thirteen he had his head shaved by Ch'an Master Shao Luan; at twenty-three he was fully ordained on (the holy mountain) Sung Yueh.

The master came to the Dharma assembly on Mt. Kuei: there he served as the rice steward. One day he was in the rice room sieving rice, when Kuei Shan said to him, "You shouldn't throw away what the donor gave us." Shih Shuang said, "I'm not throwing anything away." Kuei Shan picked up a grain of rice off the floor and said, "You said you didn't throw anything away: where did this come from?" Shih Shuang had no reply. Kuei Shan also said, "Don't slight this one grain of rice: a hundred thousand grains are born from this one grain." Shih Shuang said, "A hundred thousand grains arise from this one grain, but where does this one grain come from?" Kuei Shan laughed loudly and returned to his abbot's quarters. That night he went up to the hall and said, "(Attention) everybody! There's a worm in the rice."

Later Shih Shuang studied with Tao Wu. He asked, "What is enlightenment right before the eyes?" Tao Wu called to a novice, and the novice responded. Wu said, "Fill the water pitcher." Wu then asked Shih Shuang, "What did you just ask?" Shuang then repeated his question. Wu immediately got up and left. From this Shuang had an awakening. Tao Wu said, "I'm sick: I am about to leave the world. I have something on my mind that has been bothering me for a long time—who can clear it up?" Shuang said, "Mind and things are both wrong; trying to clear them away increases the affliction." Tao Wu said, "How sage!"

In order to shun the world, the master mixed with lay people in the Liu Yang Pottery works in Ch'ang Sha. In the mornings he wandered, in the evenings he rested. No one could become acquainted with him. Later, because Tung Shan Liang Chieh sent a monk to search him out, his talents began to be revealed, and he was chosen to reside on Shih Shuang Shan ("Stone Frost Mountain.") Later when Tao Wu was about to abandon his

congregation and die, he considered Shih Shuang his true successor, and personally went to Shih Shuang to be near him.
Shih Shuang served him scrupulously, with all the etiquette
due a teacher. After a while Tao Wu died, and disciples flocked
to Shih Shuang, forming a congregation of five hundred.

A monk asked, "What is the meaning of the coming from
the West?" The master said, "A piece of rock in empty space."
When the monk bowed, the master said, "Do you understand?"
The monk said, "I don't understand." The master said, "Luckily you don't understand. If you did it would have smashed
your head."

The master stayed at Shih Shuang for twenty years' time.
His students always sat, they never lay down. All over the
country they were known as the "dead tree congregation." The
T'ang emperor Hsi Tsung heard of the fame of the master's
Path and sent emissaries to bestow purple robes on him. The
master steadfastly refused to accept them. In 889 he showed
sickness and died at the age of eighty-two; he had been a monk
for fifty-nine years.

WEN SUI of Ch'in Shan
CASE 56

(The following is from the *Ching Te Ch'uan Teng Lu* 17)

The master was originally from Fu Chou. While still young
he was ordained by Ch'an Master Huan Chung at the Temple
of Great Compassion in Hang Chou. At the time Yen T'ou and
Hsueh Feng were in the congregation: when they saw Ch'in
Shan express his opinions, they knew he was a vessel of the
Dharma. They took him along with them as they went travelling. The affinities of these two worthies meshed with Te Shan:
each received his seal; but though Ch'in Shan was aroused
many times, in the end he was still frozen and stuck. One day
he asked Te Shan, "T'ien Huang spoke this way; Lung T'an
spoke this way; (Lung T'an was Te Shan's master; T'ien Huang
was Lung T'an's) I wonder, how does Te Shan speak?" Te Shan
said, "Try to cite what T'ien Huang and Lung T'an said." As
Ch'in Shan was about to put forward some words, Te Shan
herded him into the Nirvana Hall (i.e., the infirmary). Ch'in
Shan said, "You may be right, but you beat me too much."

Later Ch'in Shan awoke at Tung Shan's words: hence he was Tung Shan's successor. At age twenty-seven he settled at Ch'in Shan. To his congregation he related that when he first visited Tung Shan, Tung Shan asked, "Where did you come here from?" The master said, "From Great Compassion." Tung Shan said, "And did you see the master of Great Compassion?" The master said, "I did." Tung Shan said, "Did you see him before form or after form?" The master said, "It was not seeing before or after." Tung Shan was silent, so the master then said, "Having left my master too soon, I didn't get to the bottom of his meaning."

A monk asked, "What is the meaning of the coming from the West?" Ch'in Shan said, "The Lord of Liang's (Emperor Wu's) T-square, Master Chih's cutting knife."

A monk asked, "What is your family style, Teacher?" The master said, "Brocade curtains and a silver incense box: when the wind blows, the whole road is filled with perfume." Another monk asked, "How do you teach people, Teacher?" The master said, "If I taught people, I'd be the same as you lot." The monk said, "I've come especially to visit you, Teacher: you should reveal the style of the sect." The master said, "If you came specially, I'll have to." The monk said, "Please do." The master then struck him. The monk was speechless. Ch'in Shan said, "You're guarding a stump, waiting for a rabbit,* falsely using your mental spirit."

*A man who happened to see a rabbit collide with a tree stump and drop down dead foolishly sticks by the stump, waiting for it to "catch" another rabbit.

MAHASATTVA FU (497-569)
CASE 67

Mahasattva Fu, also called Shan Hui, was a layman and a small farmer; in his middle twenties he retired to a mountain with his wife and two children, where he worked during the day and practiced the Way at night. In the course of time he gave up all of his possessions three times, sold his wife and children, and hired himself out as a laborer, spending the proceeds to feed the poor and hungry. Throughout his life he continued to work, assisted by his family (who, out of respect for the Mahasattva, were not actually enslaved by their purchasers) and disciples; he fasted and gave the food saved thereby to the needy. The time during which he lived was especially bitter for great masses of peasants, and Mahasattva Fu is exemplary for his continued generosity in almsgiving, not only of Dharma, but also of material goods. He went into the capital of Liang several times to preach, hoping to spread the Dharma more widely than was possible from his mountain abode. The following is a summary of three levels of goodness, to which Fu enjoined Emperor Wu of Liang in his first letter to the monarch:

> *The highest good has an empty heart as its basis,*
> *and non-attachment as its source; abolishment of*
> *formality is the cause, and nirvana is the result.*

> *The middling good has government of oneself as its*
> *basis, and government of the nation as its source;*
> *the fruits experienced by gods and humans will be*
> *   peace and happiness.*

> *The least good is to protect and nourish living*
> *   beings,*
> *to overcome cruelty and abolish murder, and to*
> *   have all*
> *the farmers receive free food six times a month.*

Mahasattva Fu was thought to be a manifestation of Maitreya, the future Buddha.

CHIH CH'ANG of Kuei Tsung Temple
CASE 69

(The following is taken from the *Ching Te Ch'uan Teng Lu* 7)

The master went up into the Hall and said, "The ancient worthies of antiquity were not without knowledge. Those most high great men were not the same as the common sort. Right now, if you can't establish yourself independently, you're wasting your time. All of you: don't misuse your minds—there's no one to take your place, nor is there any way for you to use your minds. Don't go to others to seek. Since you've always just relied on others to understand, when they spoke you always got stuck. The fact that your light doesn't penetrate through is just because there are things before your eyes."

A monk asked, "What is the hidden meaning?" The master said, "There is no one who can understand." "What is turning towards it?" The master said, "If there is turning towards, this immediately goes against it." "What is not turning towards it?" The master said, "Who is looking for the hidden meaning?" He also said, "Go away! There's no place for you to use your mind." The monk said, "How is it you have no expedient means to enable this student to gain entry?" The master said, "The Sound-Seer's* wondrous wisdom-power can save you from the suffering of the world." "What is Kuanyin's wondrous wisdom—power?" asked the monk. The master knocked three times on the lid of the three-legged cauldron and said, "Do you hear that or not?" The monk said he did hear. The master said, "Why didn't I hear it?" The monk was speechless, so the master drove him out with blows of his staff.

Yun Yen came calling. The master made the motions of drawing a bow. Yun Yen, after a pause, made the gesture of drawing a sword. The master said, "Too late."

The master went up into the Hall and said, "Today I'm going to talk Ch'an: all of you come closer." Everyone approached, and the master said, "Listen to Kuanyin's conduct, responding well in all the various places." A monk asked, "What is Kuanyin's conduct?" The master then snapped his fingers and said, "Do all of you hear or not?" The monks said, "We hear." The master said, "What is this bunch of guys looking for here?" and drove them out with blows. Laughing loudly, he returned to his abbot's quarters.

---

* "Sound-Seer" is a translation of the name of Kuanyin, the bodhisattva of unlimited compassion, who "observes the sounds of the world."

Traditional Teaching Devices

THE THREE ROADS OF TUNG SHAN

(The following explanation is taken from Shigetsu Ein's *Funogo san ro, da, shi i rui,* a 'Non-talk on the three roads, (three) falls, and four different kinds' (1761). Shigetsu was a Soto Zen master, a Japanese descendant of Ts'ao-Tung Ch'an.)

For innumerable aeons, since there has been self, this stinking skinbag has been changed from time to time, transformed from place to place, in a thousand conditions, ten thousand forms; who can reach the realm of our fundamental quiescence?

If you get here, you must know this road. 'This road' means while dwelling in the present heap of sound and form, first getting rid of clinging to self, and attaining our former original state of selflessness. And furthermore, you must know that all things have no self. Once person and things are selfless, in your daily activities you walk in the void. This life basically has an undefiled practice and experience; thus would we practice and experience nondefilement. Today you must diligently walk in the void. Walking in the void is not some special art; each day when you go into the hall, you should not chew through a single grain of rice. Not chewing through a single grain of rice means that there is no breaking of the fast or violation of discipline by arousing mindfulness of tasting flavor. This is called traveling the bird's path.

Travel on the bird's path is trackless; when you don't leave your body in the realm of tracklessness, this is the turning point of an ascetic. After you have arrived here and settled here, there is still one road going beyond. This road is not in going or coming; it is what is called 'moss growing in the jade palace.' All the names of the Other Side are temporary names for this. In reality, it is the one road that cannot be touched upon. That is why we say 'hidden.' And 'hidden' is not a matter of giving a name as its meaning; the realm called the hidden road is the realm of no name or meaning. This is why it is said, 'He has no country; he does not abide, dwells in no home.'

To know this and yet be able to not remain here, to be an example for beings, to inspire and lead them, unify and teach them, is called 'extending the hands.' In extending the hands, there is no separate road; it does not transgress the bird's path. Traveling the bird's path by yourself, yet you extend your hands. In the bird's path there is no separate road; knowing the hidden road yourself, you still don't transgress it. Dwelling in the bird's path, you don't sprout horns on your head but always extend your hands.

Thus the three roads are the cause and effect of the great practice; and the cause and effect spreads vast and wide throughout the whole universe.

THREE KINDS OF FALL

(The following sayings are attributed to Ts'ao Shan Pen Chi, a great desciple of Tung Shan, also known as the Former Ts'ao Shan; the remarks in parenthesis may be those of Ts'ao Shan Liao Wu, known as Great Master Hui Hsia, a successor of Pen Chi, known as the second generation Ts'ao Shan. There is a certain amount of confusion as to the authorship of some early Ts'ao-Tung works, but this is totally irrelevant to our purpose.)

An ascetic taking food has three kinds of fall: being a water buffalo is the fall of an ascetic; not accepting food is the fall of the precious; not cutting off sound and form is the fall according to kind. Just fall; whose business is this?

(If you want to know, this is going in among different kinds, not approving the business of asceticism, purification, and tranquilization. Therefore the Ancients provisionally used the water buffalo to represent different kinds. But these are different kinds in terms of phenomena, not speech.)

As for different kinds of speech, all speech back and forth is of a kind; that is why Nan Ch'uan said, "Where knowledge cannot reach, just don't speak of it; if you speak of it, then horns will grow on your head. Even if you call it 'thus,' already it has changed. You should just go work among different kinds of beings." Right now you must go into differentiation and speak of the phenomena in differentiation; only when there are no words in your words will you be able to do so. When Nan Ch'uan was ailing, someone asked, "Master, after you die,

where will you go?" Ch'uan said, "I'll be a water buffalo at the
house of the patron down the mountain." His questioner said,
"I want to accompany you, master, but can I?" Ch'uan said, "If
you follow me, come with a blade of grass in your mouth."

(These are words of an ascetic transforming himself; therefore he says, 'If you want to approach, come with a blade of
grass in your mouth.' To approach intimately is called 'Only
nonattachment is worthy of offering.')

He also said, "As for the fall according to kind, right now in
the midst of all sounds and forms, to turn oneself around on
everything and not fall into gradations is called falling according to kind."

He also said, "As for the fall of the precious, the body of
reality and nature of reality are precious things; they too must
be turned around—this is the fall of the precious. Right now,
the White Ox on Open Ground is the ultimate model of the
body of reality; it too must be turned around, so that one may
avoid sitting in the region of uniformity with no discrimination. This is also called the business of cutting off offering. If
you want to use offerings, you must obtain this food. Thus it is
called flavorless flavor, and it is called nonattachment being
worthy of offering. All the rest is defiled food; it is not the food
of nonattached liberation. Someone asked Pai Chang, 'What is
used for food?' Pai Chang said, 'Nonattachment is used for
food.' Yun Yen said, 'Do not use flavor for offerings.' Tao Wu
said, 'Knowing there exists something to maintain, all is offering.'"

Those who take food from correct livelihood must have all
three kinds of fall.

At the time, a monk asked, "Wearing fur and horns—what
fall is this? Not accepting food—what fall is this? Not cutting
off sound and form—what fall is this?" I said, "Wearing fur and
horns is the fall of the ascetic. Not cutting off sound and form
is the fall according to kind. Not accepting food is the fall of the
precious—this is the fundamental thing; one knows it exists,
yet does not grasp it, so it is said, 'fall of the precious.' As for
wearing fur and horns, the fall of an ascetic, this is not clinging
to the business of asceticism, nor to the states of rewards of all
saints. As for not cutting off sound and form, the fall according
to kind, because a beginner knows he has his own fundamental
thing, when he turns back the light he gets rid of all form,

sound, smell, flavor, feel, and ideas, and attains stillness. Thus after he perfects this accomplishment, he does not cling to the six sense fields; falling among them, he is not befuddled, going along with them without hindrance. Therefore it is said, 'The six teachers of outside paths are your teachers; when those teachers fall, you also fall along with them, and thereby can eat.' The food is the food of right livelihood; it is also the fundamental thing. It is just that not being defiled by the perceptive awareness in your six senses is called 'falling'—it is not the same as former fears. One does not even grasp his own concern, the fundamental thing, much less anything else.''

THE FIVE STATES OF LORD AND VASSAL

(The germ of the five states—or positions, ranks—is in the Ts'an T'ung Ch'i, 'Merging of Difference and Identity,' written by Shih T'ou (700–790), ancestor of the Ts'ao-Tung house. Tung Shan exposed the five states in his Pao Ching San Mei Ke, 'Song of the Jewel Mirror Meditation,' and composed a set of poems on the five states of the interrelation of the true/ absolute and biased/relative. Ts'ao Shan, who seems to have used the five ranks more than Tung Shan's other disciples, had been a scholar of Confucianism until the age of nineteen and expressed the five states in terms of lord and vassal, or prince and minister. The following is Ts'ao Shan's explanation.)

The absolute state is the realm of emptiness, where there has never been a single thing; the relative state is the realm of form, with myriad forms. The relative within the absolute is turning away from principle and going to phenomena; the absolute within the relative is indifference to phenomena, entering principle. Mutual integration is subtly responding to myriad circumstances without falling into various existences. It is not defiled, not pure, not true, not biased; therefore it is called the empty mysterious great way, the non-grasping true source. The past worthies since time immemorial have esteemed this rank (state of integration) as the most wondrous and most mysterious. You must discern it clearly and thoroughly. The lord is the absolute state, the vassal is the relative state. The vassal turning towards the lord is the absolute within the relative; the lord looking upon the vassal is the relative within the absolute. The way of lord and vassal in harmony is an expression of mutual integration.

A monk asked, "What is the lord like?"

The master said, "His wondrous virtue is honored throughout the world; his lofty illumination shines through the great void."

"What is the vassal like?"

"His spiritual activity spreads the holy way; true wisdom benefits living beings."

"What is the vassal turning towards the lord?"

"Without falling into various dispositions, freezing his feelings he gazes upon the holy countenance."

"What is the lord looking at the vassal?"

"Although his wondrous countenance doesn't move, the shining of his light is fundamentally without bias."

"What is the way of lord and vassal in harmony?"

"Comingling, without inside or outside; merging harmoniously, with upper and lower equal."

FEN YANG ON THE FIVE STATES

(Fen Yang Shan Chao, 947–1024, was one of the great ancestors of the Lin Chi house of Ch'an, noteworthy for his development of the *kung an* as a tool in Ch'an study; one of his points was to show the unity of the essence of Ch'an in the midst of the various methods which had evolved in the streams of Ch'an teaching over the preceding three hundred years.)

Coming from within the absolute

> *The jewel sword of the diamond king*
> *Sweeps the skies with a spiritual light;*
> *It shines freely throughout the world, like a crystal,*
> *Its clear radiance free of dust.*

The relative within the absolute (biased within the true)

> *The thunderous roar of cutting dynamism—*
> *To watch for the sparks and lightning*
> *Is still dull thinking;*
> *Hesitate and you are a thousand mountains away.*

The absolute within the relative (true within the biased)

> See the wheel-turning king;
> Enforcing the true imperative, with seven regal
>   treasures and a thousand sons.
> Everything accompanies him on the road,
> Still he seeks a golden mirror.

Arriving in both (in old tradition, this is arriving in the relative/biased)

> A three year old golden lion;
> His teeth and claws are all there—
> All demons and apparitions
> Faint at the sound of his roar.

Simultaneous realization of both

> Great glory is effortless;
> Quit making a wooden ox walk.
> The real one goes through the fire—
> The wonder of wonders of the King of Dharma.

Coming from within the absolute is lotus flowers blooming on parched ground—their golden calyxes and silver stems are bathed in jade dewdrops. The eminent monk does not sit on the phoenix pedestal. The relative within the absolute—the moon is bright at midnight, the sun must greet the dawn. The absolute within the relative—a hair tip becomes a huge tree, a drop of water becomes a river. Arriving in both—spirit does not come from heaven or earth; how can heroism depend on the four seasons for its impulse? Simultaneous realization—the jade woman casts the shuttle on the whirring loom, the stone man beats the drum, boom boom.

FEN YANG'S EIGHTEEN TYPES OF QUESTIONS

(This list is taken from the *Jen T'ien Yen Mu*, 'Eye of Humans and Gods,' and it seems that the examples given are not necessarily chosen by Fen Yang Shan Chao himself.)

asking for instruction—a monk asked Ma Tsu, "What is Buddha?" Ma Tsu said, "Mind is Buddha." Chao Chou said, "The one in the shrine."

presenting one's understanding—a monk asked Lung Ya, "How is it when 'sky cannot cover, earth cannot hold'?" Lung Ya said, "People of the way should be like this."

investigating and discerning—someone asked Lin Chi, "The student has a question; how is it when it is on the part of the teacher?" Lin Chi said, "Say it quickly! Tell me right away!" As the student hesitated to speak, Lin Chi struck him.

meeting of minds—a monk asked T'ien Huang, "What about when the feeling of doubt has not subsided?" T'ien Huang said, "Sticking to one is not real."

wrapping up (focusing)—a monk asked Pa Chiao, "The whole earth is an eye; I ask the teacher's guidance." Pa Chiao said, "A poor man comes upon a feast."

mental activity—a monk asked Hsing Hua, "I cannot distinguish black from white; I ask the teacher to help me." Hua hit him as he spoke.

seeking out—someone asked Feng Hsueh, "Why does someone who does not understand not doubt?" Hsueh said, "When the sacred tortoise crawls overland how can it avoid leaving tracks in the mud?"

not understanding—a monk asked Hsuan Sha, "The student has just entered the monastery; please show me an entry road." Hsuan Sha said, "Do you hear the sound of the valley stream?" "Yes," answered the monk. Sha said, "Enter from there."

lifting up—someone asked an old adept, "'Wordly knowledge and brilliant intellect should not be brought out at all'— return the words to me." The adept immediately hit him.

posing a question—someone asked Yun Men, "What about when you don't see any boundaries when looking directly?" Yun Men said, "Reflect."

intentional question—someone asked Shou Shan, "All sentient beings have the Buddha nature—why don't they know it?" Shou Shan said, "They know."

using things/events—someone asked Feng Hsueh, "There is a pearl in the sea; how can I get it?" "When Wang Hsiang arrives, the light shines; where Li Lou goes, the waves flood the skies." (Wang Hsiang and Li Lou were legendary men of supernormal eyesight: the former once found a lost pearl for the Yellow Emperor of high antiquity.)

real question—someone asked San Sheng, "I only see that you are a monk; what are the Buddha and the Teachings?" San Sheng said, "This is Buddha, this is the Teaching; do you know it?"

fabricated question—someone asked Ching Shan, "This here is the one in the shrine—what is the Buddha?" Ching Shan said, "This is the one in the shrine."

making sure—someone asked one of the ancestral teachers, "All things fundamentally are existent—what is nonexistent?" The Patriarch said, "Your question is quite clear; why bother to ask further of me?"

eliciting—someone asked Mu Chou, "What did the ancestral teacher Bodhidharma come from India to China for?" Mu Chou said, "You tell me what it's for." The monk did not reply, so Mu Chou hit him.

clarifying (the example given is the main case of *The Blue Cliff Record* 65)

silent question—an outsider came to the Buddha and stood there silently in his presence. The Buddha said, "So much." The outsider said, "World Honored One, your great mercy and compassion have allowed me to enter."